"Jake Hamilton has been used by
of Christ and in my personal life
like. This book will be a sword in
to be all that God has called hin

Brian Barcelona, speaker and author, *The Jesus Club*
and *Don't Scroll*

"Jake Hamilton creatively blends the wisdom of Jesus' teachings, ancient wisdom traditions, and Parzival's quest for the Holy Grail to address the modern crisis in masculinity. This book offers a vital, holistic journey, redefining manhood away from toxic stereotypes and guiding men through their God-intended, heroic paths in family and society."

Bishop Mark J. Chironna, PhD, founding and lead pastor, Church On The Living Edge; founder, Mark Chironna Ministries; presiding bishop, Legacy Edge Alliance

"If you build it, He (the Father) will come. Jake Hamilton's powerful and practical, sensitive and compassionate book on building men and fathers is a major impetus to the fulfillment of the ultimate 'field of dreams,' bringing many sons to glory."

Lou Engle, founder of TheCall and Bound4LIFE

"A book filled with wit, wisdom, and invitation. Hamilton offers a robust path to a deeper life, and he does so with great gusto. As readers, we have a lively guide at our arm, even as the darkness gathers."

Dr. Martin Shaw, author and teacher

"In *The Journey to Biblical Masculinity*, Jake Hamilton reacquaints us with Jesus as the paragon of manliness and reacclimatizes our imaginations toward a model of manhood men were both designed and destined for."

Jason Upton, songwriter, speaker, and worship leader

"Now more than ever in our history, the power and importance of biblical masculinity cannot be overstated. In this book, you will experience the transformational power of storytelling to unlock the hearts of men and thus transform the heart of our culture. You will be infused with the courage to pursue your own journey and reap the benefits for years to come!"

Kris Vallotton, cofounder, Bethel School of Supernatural Ministry; author, *Spiritual Intelligence* and *Uprising*

The Journey to Biblical Masculinity

The Journey to Biblical Masculinity

12 Paths Every Man Must Take

Jake Hamilton

Chosen

a division of Baker Publishing Group

ChosenBooks.com

Published by Chosen Books
Minneapolis, Minnesota
ChosenBooks.com

Chosen Books is a division of
Baker Publishing Group, Grand Rapids, Michigan

Printed in the United States of America

Library of Congress Cataloging-in-Publication Data
Names: Hamilton, Jake (Musician), author.
Title: The journey to biblical masculinity : 12 paths every man must take / Jake
    Hamilton.
Description: Minneapolis, Minnesota : Chosen Books, a division of Baker
    Publishing Group, [2024] | Includes bibliographical references.
Identifiers: LCCN 2023049531 | ISBN 9780800772581 (paper) | ISBN 9780800772598
    (casebound) | ISBN 9781493445707 (ebook)
Subjects: LCSH: Men--Biblical teaching. | Masculinity—Biblical teaching. |
    Christian men.
Classification: LCC BS2545.M39 H36 2024 | DDC 248.8/42—dc23/eng/20240213
LC record available at https://lccn.loc.gov/2023049531

Cover Design: Studio Gearbox

Baker Publishing Group publications use paper produced from sustainable forestry practices and postconsumer waste whenever possible.

24 25 26 27 28 29 30   7 6 5 4 3 2 1

To my wife, Nicci,

whose patient endurance with my growth has allowed me to become the man I am today and our marriage to flourish into the love story we have today. You are intuitive and brave, always ready for a fun adventure, and willing to dive into other people's pain to help them discover what's hindering them from being their truest self. I am undone by your beauty every single day, and I am forever in your debt for the love you have so graciously offered me, as well as your unrelenting devotion to our family regardless of how hard the season is. It is a privilege to be your husband.

To my daughter, Geneva,

your life has become my greatest teacher, your smile my greatest inspiration. You perfectly set the pace of our home, and I am forever humbled and grateful that I get the privilege of being your father.

To my son Ezra,

you are all my heart without any of my pain. You bleed the very beauty of creation itself, committed to craft, empathetic and helpful, gifted and so much fun. It is my honor to be your father.

To my son Judah,

you are all my passion and all my devotion, without any of my failures. You are a beautiful and courageous picture of masculinity, creative and fearless, kind and merciful. It is my honor to be your father.

Contents

Acknowledgments

It is without a doubt a reality that this book would not exist without the following works. First, Martin Shaw's *Snowy Tower*, the only other purely narrative version of Wolfram von Eschenbach's *Parzival* I could find, from one of the greatest storytellers on earth today. Shaw's work has inspired my retelling of the story around campfires with groups of men, as well as inspiring the written form you will find within these pages. Also Robert A. Johnson's book *He: Understanding Masculine Psychology*, which followed Chrétien de Troyes's "Perceval: The Story of the Grail" version and gives psychological insight into it, following in the footsteps of Carl Jung's work on the story and on the subject of mythology in the role of psychological development.

This, of course, leads me to mention the great work done by Emma Jung and Marie-Louise von Franz titled *The Grail Legend*, which takes thirty years of research into the story of Parzival and offers it to us in a writing masterpiece that will outlive us all. I also referenced *The Parzival of Wolfram von Eschenbach*, Wolfram's Germanic version of the story as translated by Edwin H. Zeydel, in collaboration with Bayard Quincy Morgan, if you would enjoy reading the three hundred plus pages of the original version in poetic verse. And finally, Father Richard Rohr's catalogue of books on masculinity and male rites of passage: *The Quest for the Grail*, and *From Wild Man to Wise Man*, and also *Adam's Return*.

These books gave me permission to explore the connection between my faith and my formation as a man. Any references or quotes that I may have thought were mine, but were formed by these works, I want to recognize here. Any unintentional claims to original thoughts that find their root systems in these works, I want to honestly admit. The last five years have been devoted to this work, and somewhere along the way you lose the ability to distinguish between the fruit and its root system. I am grateful for these works and so many more that have inspired my effort here and the man I am today.

Introduction

The Heroic Image of True Masculinity

Every little boy wants to be the hero of his story, from the moment he picks up his first stick and pretends it's a sword.

For me, a child in the late 1980s, I wanted to be a Thunder-Cat. "*Thunder. Thunder. ThunderCats Hoooooooooo!*" roared Lion-O every Saturday morning. I waited eagerly for the next story, the next moment of courage, the next moment of adventure to take me beyond my experience and deep into the recesses of my imagination. I was hooked. I eventually got into comic books, probably more than most. I didn't collect comics for saving and investment. I was an artist. I copied the characters, tore out the pages, and savored all the stories. I had all the toys and tried to save up for anything I could get—every vehicle, character, and lair, until I had the craziest thought: *What if I drew my own comics?*

I could draw and design my own adventures and make my own stories come to life.

So, I did.

I drew my first comic, or at least my first attempt at one, when I was about ten years old. I called it *The Masked Avenger.*

It was full of characters and action, dynamic conflict and romance. Even though I was only ten, it allowed me to make myself into the main character and play out the fantasy of the hero who saves the world. I designed a comic book where I was the hero—every boy's dream and every man's desire.

But it's more than just a dream or a desire.

It's the invitation of heaven.

The Creator called me by name and initiated our joint story, giving me the opportunity to partner with Him and co-create while I am still alive amidst my own broken, dysfunctional, no-hope story. In fact, such characters seem to be the ones He uses the most. I didn't grow up in a perfect family, in a perfect neighborhood, with perfect parents, because that doesn't exist for anyone. Are some stories harder than others? Of course they are, but that's the beauty of a good story. Can you imagine watching a movie where nothing ever goes wrong, and the heroes never have a moment where they can't seem to win because all the odds are stacked against them? *Boring.*

In fact, let me give it to you in another way: we all learn the most through the trying and difficult seasons of our lives.

Nobody learns anything in seasons of comfort and tranquility.

When our weakness is exposed, our vulnerability is revealed, we learn more about ourselves and others than at any other point in our story. There are lots of reasons why we avoid these seasons, even though they're when we learn the most. In fact, this is why heroes are still needed. We need pioneers and adventurers who aren't afraid of the hard stuff to show us that we can make it through, and to call us from the other side into greater levels of courage.

The prophet Daniel says in essence that those who know their God will have great adventures: "But the people who know their God shall be strong and do great things" (Daniel 11:32 TLB). This shows us that the courage we desire isn't found in a personality trait; it's found through relational encounters with our Creator. These encounters don't have to be profound or monumental experiences; they can be quiet, understated moments where you grow in your connection to the Divine and draw deeper into the depths of relationship. From that place, your adventures begin to unfold right in front of you.

These adventures are grounded in everyday, ordinary life choices, standing our ground against all odds for marriage, family, and the Kingdom of God. As men, we have something inside us that wants to be king of the mountain, captain of the football team, rock star, leader, dragon slayer. When that's missing, we know it's a sign that something has been broken, something has been lost inside the boy.

That doesn't mean every man needs to be aggressive, loud, extroverted, or obnoxious. It means that within each young boy there is the spark of courage and the ability to defend that which he claims to love. That was what I discovered in my comic book–fueled imagination. I believed that if given an opportunity, I would have been able to seize it, rise to the occasion, and become the man I daydreamed about, bold and fearless. But in life, if that moment doesn't come quickly enough or in the way we thought it would, we begin trying to force it on an unsuspecting population ourselves. Our desires and design don't change, but our opportunities to express them do.

The brutality of this is revealed in young boys who grow up to be men who were never given the opportunity to use their powers for good, so they often use them for evil. Men who were kind become cold and hard. Men who were generous become selfish. Men who were compassionate leaders turn into controlling rebels. Men who were humble become egomaniacs. Men who had a heart for justice begin to oppress and enslave. Men who had a prophetic leading become manipulating.

Men who were encouragers begin to use their words to damage and abuse.

This happens to the best of us. Look at the life of the ancient King David, who ruled Israel between 1010 and 970 BC. He was considered a good man who led better than had his predecessor, and he would go on to be known as a man after the Creator's own heart. His life was lived in such proximity to the One who created him that he actually took on His likeness in the way he led as a king and lived as a man. But we all have weaknesses, and this is why, although we may love our Creator, believe in His Son, and be filled with the Spirit, we still fall. We are dependent beings.

As for King David, after leading many years and fighting many wars, he was found in a compromising situation. God's Word, the Bible, says that in a day when kings were supposed to be at war, David was at home. One night, he found himself on his balcony, staring at someone else's wife while she was bathing. I tend to think that if he had had a computer, David would have had massive struggles with pornography. Once he saw her, he then used his ability to mobilize armies and conquer kingdoms to manipulate one woman and overthrow one family. He took another man's wife as his own, abducted her, raped her, lied about it, and then had her husband killed (see 2 Samuel 11). This can become the path of all good, well-intentioned men who don't understand the nature of their masculinity and the very real war they are currently fighting.

Have you ever noticed that *evil* spelled backward is *live*? To truly be alive, to *live*, is the exact opposite of *evil*. I believe that if we lose our vision to live in the fullness we were created for, we will default to evil behaviors. It is time to break those chains and find the hero inside us, placed there by our Creator. It is time to live with purpose, with clarity. To *live* is to come home, to be intentional with our time and talents and treasures, to waste nothing we have for selfish gain. Like David, we were made for war, but we keep finding ourselves scrolling for attention and definition. Even the gentlest and most artistic men were made to go to battle for that which we claim to love.

The difference is expression, not design or desire. Some men may lead campaigns or missions to foreign lands, while others may write the songs that fuel these movements and paint paintings that show the depth and color of all the Creator is doing. They may also expose the world's evils through every frame of the camera or stroke of the brush. It is time for heroes to rise again and display who they are with conviction. You can't have heroes without conflict, but our battle is not against flesh and blood. Real heroes in this hour don't need swords and shields or mechanical armor and magic hammers; they need character and integrity that display the power of manhood to transform the planet in a world of sexual chaos and inconsistent values.

That's who I am writing to—men who need to know there is hope and that they can make it and become the men they were created to be. Men who have already messed it up, and men who are just a few steps away from blowing their lives up. Men who are just starting to feel something is off, and men burned out from all these conversations.

I am also writing this for the heroes who already exist out there. Men who have endured hardship and loss, or who have experienced addiction and adultery, and have chosen the better path. They have chosen not to walk away from it all, not to buy into the lies of the culture and the pressures of the age, and not to throw their lives, families, and futures in the trash for a lesser thing.

But most importantly and selfishly, I am writing this book as a letter to my sons, for my future heroes, and for their journey. I can't tell them, or you, all the pitfalls and blind spots that exist. All I can offer is what I've found and what the Creator mentions in His Word. Once my boys hit their preteen years, I realized I had no idea how to walk them from boyhood to manhood—despite years of Bible training and full-time Christian ministry. I bought bestselling books people recommended, I knew Bible verses I should sow into their lives, and I had some personal experience that could translate into teachable moments. But our time together started to sound as if we were at a Christian conference, not like a dad connecting with his sons' hearts in a way that would impact their view of masculinity and their role as men in the world.

So I began to explore ancient rites of passage for young men, and the stories that were shared to guide them through the experience. These stories became a key to unlocking my sons' hearts, and mine as well. I could see why men throughout history sat in circles around a fire and told heroic tales of epic journeys. Such tales became a way to view my life, my experience, and my faults, without shame, without consequence. I could see each character and his journey as a picture of my own, and in that place, I understood why it says in two of the four Gospels that Jesus never taught without telling what could be called a "fake story." Some people prefer the word *parable*, but in ancient tradition, both in the Church and in culture, it's called *myth*—a story rooted in the culture it came from, so deep and profound that it leads us to the truth we have been looking for the whole time.

In recent years, we've allowed masculinity to be defined by those who have been hurt the most by its destructive and oppressive nature. But that's not everyone's experience, it's not historically and sociologically accurate, and it's definitely not biblically and mythologically the whole truth. We must come up with working definitions for masculinity, male spirituality, and male rites of passage that allow boys to have a vision for their personal and spiritual journey, while giving adult males the opportunity to see when they are falling short of their God-given potential.

Without these definitions and psychological and spiritual structures, working out what it means to be a man and how men ought to behave becomes a free-for-all. At that point, culture defines the masculine through media and leaves us with socio-pathic or paralyzed versions where men don't know whether or not they're allowed to pay for dinner on a date, open the car door for a woman, work hard at their job to provide for a family, or simply stay home with the kids. In this type of culture, any act of aggression is proof of toxic masculinity, and any form of male-dominated leadership is patriarchal. There must be a better way, a pathway that leads us through the wilderness of social constructs and theological ideas and offers us something firm to stand on and a clear vision for the future.

The answer is *story*.

In our modern society, with tweets and blogs, podcasts and Substack, we forget that most of our psychological and theological DNA has primarily been passed on through oral tradition. And it wasn't informational; it was mythological. Storytelling wasn't about passing on the rules of a culture, but the heart of a culture. Then through the doorway of the heart, those who heard these stories were able to see what was expected of them and the potential blessings and consequences of their actions played out in fantastic narrative, engaging their divine imagination and the simplest and truest parts of their nature.

A story is a way we can view the world and our experience in it. Rarely, if ever, do we see things as they truly are. We see things through the lens of our experience, our pain, our victory, our passions, our personality. That's why we need the cooperative power of mythological and personal stories in our life. Myths speak to the larger tribal narrative of human experience, and personal stories apply to our everyday experiences in life.

Before you question the validity of using mythology to discover eternal truths, look at the life of Jesus. I mentioned earlier that the Gospels say twice that Jesus never taught without using a "fake story." What is a fake story but a myth? We just like the word *parable* because we so appreciate religious language. But our historic, tribal, and oral tradition would have called Jesus' parables *myths*, shared them around campfires, and embraced that they were more than they appeared on the surface. We might even use the word *prophetic* here. They were prophetic stories giving us insight into eternal realities grounded in the everyday world we inhabit.

Look at how the prophet Nathan confronted King David when David was in the most vulnerable and rebellious moments of his life. He had sinned by committing adultery and then having the husband of the woman he slept with killed on the front lines of battle, while he rested at home. David knew what he did was wrong, but the prophet Nathan didn't confront him with the direct truth of his actions. By telling David a story, Nathan gave him the dignity of discovering the truth for himself:

> "There were two men in a certain town, one rich and the other poor. The rich man had a very large number of sheep and cattle, but the poor man had nothing except one little ewe lamb he had bought. He raised it, and it grew up with him and his children. It shared his food, drank from his cup and even slept in his arms. It was like a daughter to him.
>
> Now a traveler came to the rich man, but the rich man refrained from taking one of his own sheep or cattle to prepare a meal for the traveler who had come to him. Instead, he took the ewe lamb that belonged to the poor man and prepared it for the one who had come to him."
>
> 2 Samuel 12:1–4 NIV

The Bible says that David "burned with anger" against the rich man in the story (verse 5). He demanded justice for the poor man whose sheep had been stolen, because David had not yet put together that *he* was that rich man. But once he connected the dots through Nathan's declaration "You are the man!" (verse 7), he was able to repent and begin the process of transformation.

I have written this book to help men in such a process of transformation, on their journey toward wholeness in body, mind, soul, and spirit. *The Journey to Biblical Masculinity* is a book that offers you, the reader, the opportunity to explore what it means to be a man, as well as exploring the long-lost traditions of male initiation.

Along our paths ahead, we will answer questions like "When does a boy become a man?" and "How do I help my sons become men if I never had a father to help me?" Men seem more confused than ever about how to express their masculinity in ways that offer support and courage to those in both their homes and communities.

In *The Journey to Biblical Masculinity*, I use the ancient story of "Parzival and the Quest for the Holy Grail," written in the first quarter of the thirteenth century, to uncover powerful biblical truths and serve as a framework to mark "pathways" on the journey from boyhood to manhood. These pathways include exploring *family, wilderness, adventure, aggression, mentorship, failure, grief*, and *redemption* to discover what it means to be a man, a husband, and a father. Each path we will travel is not a means to an end, but is a simple signpost on the walk of life, urging us forward to deeper places of growth, while reminding us that we aren't lost even when we fall or when the road gets rough.

My goal is to help you feel empowered and seen as you read through this story, and then to help you engage with your own story, facing every hardship and disappointment with a deep sense of hope and purpose. To facilitate the process, each chapter or path is followed by a section called "The Work," in which I invite you to explore how you are processing the concepts we talk about and how you can apply them practically to your everyday life.

This road is not easy. It is a journey into spaces of deep longing, fear, pain, loss, and regret—muddled with relentless hope, unceasing joy, and great courage. I believe in you. You are not alone as you travel it.

Path 1

Departing Business as Usual

> Here begin the terrors. Here begin the marvels.
>
> —Chrétien de Troyes,
> "Perceval: The Story of the Grail"

You are not alone.

Although your life may make you feel differently, *you are not alone*.

There are thousands of men all over the planet longing to answer foundational questions about their lives and their existence in the world. They want to know who they are and what significant role they are supposed to play. They are frustrated with their failed attempts to learn why they react and respond the way they do. They want to serve Jesus and connect in Christian community, but they feel like the outsider, the fraud, or the only one in the room who doesn't "get it." And ultimately, they want to understand what it actually means to be a husband, a father, and a son. But deeper inside them, there is a desire to know what it means to be a man. They know somehow, subconsciously, in an eternal part of them, that if they can answer that question, it is a key to unlocking the answers to all the other questions they are asking.

Ancient cultures would have prepared a man for this from the time he was born. He would have grown up in the midst of a tribe of men reminding its young boys that they were unready for the call of manhood until they had reached certain markers and completed certain tasks. Manhood required a sacred wounding that they had yet to obtain and could only attempt if they lived within the clear boundaries set around them and if they were willing to be tempered by the process. This was an invitation to a young boy, not a rejection of him. Every day that he witnessed the tribe's celebration of its men who so selflessly provided for and protected the family and friends he loved so dearly, the model of success was formed in him. The boy admired these men and hungered to be like them. They were fierce and focused, devoted and determined, merciful and sacrificial all at the same time.

But young men of this modern age are left to wander aimlessly, frustrated and confused, angry and bitter because this passage into manhood was never offered to them. They have grown up in an environment with no model of manhood from a father who loved them, chose them, and called them into masculinity's deep waters, staying by their side as they floundered repeatedly and almost drowned, as they learned to balance their own weight within the murky waters of the world around them.

Fatherhood has been abandoned for comfort and convenience, for unsustainable models of success, in the name of meeting our needs, while abandoning the needs of the children we leave behind. Young boys are therefore left to find their own rites of passage. With no older men sacrificing to guide them, they settle for violence, for sexual exploits or sexual confusion, for lazy, depressed lifestyles without any vision, because they have nothing and no one to look up to except their peers.

Maybe this is why so many of us feel alone.

We were never given the model of manhood, let alone the method of how to walk it out for a lifetime and then give our children something to look up to and live up to.

But there is an opportunity to change that.

No story is so far gone that redemption is not available.

Not one life in all of creation is so lost that it cannot be found again.

There is hope.

You are not alone.

A Working Definition of a Man

We can make powerful decisions today that will require sacrifice and suffering, but that will also develop the courage, confidence, and character in us that we know we are capable of. This will not happen overnight. If you are looking for a quick fix or a shortcut, you won't find it on the pathway to manhood. Men know how to embrace the work necessary to develop the skills and strengths required for the task ahead of them. Therefore, a working definition of what it means to be a man is required so we can find common ground and define attainable goals.

So let's begin with these few things in mind: that a man is a biologically male human who confidently chooses to go first in any circumstance and joyfully commits to honoring God, respecting women, and protecting children at all costs.

Men do this by engaging in the story they were given, not the story they wish they had. They do this by embracing tension and mystery in the face of uncertainty, and by honoring ceremony and tradition while others throw those away without concern for the sacrifices of the men who went before them.

Men do this by developing a healthy understanding of their sexuality and their sexual desires.

Men also understand the value of their emotions and know where to place them and when to express them. They do not shy away from danger. They do not abandon their families. They know the meaning of love and the value of communication. They do not start fights, but are strong enough to take a punch if one comes their way. They provide for the family and community they came from without question, and without the need for appreciation. They know what they are afraid of, but they move forward regardless so that fear doesn't define them.

A man has no use for the approval of others, as long as he can see it in the eyes of the woman he loves. His greatest joy is not what he can buy for his children, but the legacy of the life he models for them every day. A man who has woken up to his masculinity longs for more than just Bible studies and accountability groups, Sunday services and stadium gatherings. All these valuable things have a place in our expression of faith, but they will never be enough to fulfill the true desire of a man's soul because any man who has encountered Jesus Christ wants to live like Him and look like Him. A man who has had an encounter with the living God lives his devotion every day by sacrificing for his bride and calling his children to something bigger than their ego pursuits. He sees in Jesus' life more than just oversimplified theologies and religious jargon; he sees something worth living for, fighting for, and dying for.

This is a man.

Yet he feels lonely because he sees so few running into the battle with him. He wants to be called to this standard of mature masculinity, yet he shies away when he feels misunderstood.

He doesn't need to fly three thousand miles around the world to preach to strangers in order to fulfill what God has called him to. A man doesn't need religious validation from Christian institutions that would tell him his ministry is anywhere outside his own home. He walks out biblical masculinity every day when he walks thirty feet across his own living room to put his arms around his wife or to sit on the floor and play with his children.

Choosing Jesus as Our Model

This is the model of Jesus: He left His heavenly position to partner in the suffering of His Bride for the sake of her redemption. We call this *incarnation*. An embodied Christianity lived out even when it is inconvenient or uncomfortable, not just talked about with oversimplified language and theological rhetoric. Jesus would do it for the one, without the possibility for wealth or fame or even acknowledgement.

So you have to decide: *What model will you choose?*

Your birth father?

Your stepfather?

Your uncle?

Your grandfather?

Your pastor?

Your leader?

Your mentor?

I don't care how beautiful or brilliant any of these men are (or were); they are not and can never be Jesus. Their model can point you or me there, but if we are to become who we were meant to become, if we are to attain the call and the standard we were created for, then we need the model of Jesus as a man—not just as God, but as a flesh-and-blood male human.

When we choose to make Jesus our model for life, for manhood, letting His life define what it means to be a father and a husband, there is so much we must learn and so much more we must let go of. It's not as simple as a checklist or a mantra, although I wish it were. It becomes a constant turning over and over of what I thought my life was about, what I thought I stood for, and what I am currently doing, comparing these to the light of His presence and His standard for living.

This has several implications for us as men. First, *men must go first*. When we initially hear this statement, we agree, and then we immediately make it about systems and structures, platforms and positions that have nothing to do with the model of Jesus. He left His position and came to serve His Bride, the Church (see Isaiah 49:1–7; Ephesians 5:25–27; Revelation 19:6–10). He sacrificed for her to come into her fullness, even when the ones He came to save rejected and crucified Him. In the midst of His pain, He cried out that His people be forgiven. He desired to see those He loved given opportunity for redemption, regardless of His experience.

This brings us to the second implication of Jesus as our model: *Suffering is not optional; it's necessary.* You can say that you would choose your wife, love your kids, and stand up for Christ. Yet when you don't get what you want, when things don't go your way, when pain enters the story, and when sacrifice is the only way forward, will you choose to sacrifice, or will you run?

This is where the proverbial "rubber meets the road." I can have great theology, perfect habits, a thriving church community, the kids, the wife, the dog, the cars, the house, all of it . . . and then sickness, then pain, then sin, then heartbreak . . . and the question is, *Then what?*

Reaching this point is not a sign of God's frustration toward you or His abandonment of your story. It's an invitation into the depths of His heart, an initiatory moment in a man's life where he has to back up what he says he believes, regardless of whether or not he can see any value in it today. Nobody gets frustrated with a fruit tree for not blooming in winter, which is an expected cycle of life. It's a death we can see and still know that the dormant tree without any signs of life is waiting for the warmth of spring to come again. Then it will bear the fruit it was made to bear in due season. Just as no one who has read the entirety of the Gospel account gets angry when Jesus is nailed to the cross. We know what's happening next. We know what's coming.

Death is not the end of the story.

And this will land us in the third and final takeaway from the life of Jesus as a model of masculinity. This third implication may be the most difficult to live out. When Jesus becomes our model, *as men we are no longer allowed to say that our current situation, our circumstance, our sacrifice, and our suffering isn't "fair."* The most unfair act in all of human history was God wrapped in flesh hanging from a tree, put there by those He created and came to love. But that one sacrifice was redemption for all stories, for all humanity, for all time. In our homes, with our families, in the midst of our communities, we have the opportunity and the privilege to put this on display every day—but most especially when we are feeling as if we are dying, and that death is at the hands of those we love and those who claimed to love us.

Once Jesus conquered death, it went from being an enemy to being an ally. We no longer have to fear or run from death anywhere in our lives; it is an invitation to resurrection. We're not just speaking in the realm of physical death, but the death of things we loved, positions we cherished, health we thought would never fail, relationships that didn't go the way we planned, loved ones who rejected us, mentors who failed us. These are all deaths, opportunities to stop looking at life one-dimensionally and see the depth of what's available to us through Christ's example. We don't simply give up or run away when things get hard and death knocks on our door. We engage with it and explore it for divine paths of growth and resurrection.

You are not a victim of your own life.

We live in a culture where if anything doesn't go my way, or if I'm not treated the way I feel I should be treated, then I'm allowed and encouraged to throw it under the label of victimization. You and I are not the victims of someone else's bad behavior. That person might be toxic, or might be a narcissist, or might just be an ego-driven, selfish jerk, but we can choose to leave. We can find a new job, get new friends, go to a different church. Whatever it is, whomever it is, you and I have control.

You are not a victim. You probably made some destructive or poor choices yourself, and men must learn to own their junk and take responsibility for their choices and actions. This is a massive marker of maturity in a man's life—when he can see the choices he has made, recognize how they have affected his life and the lives of those around him, and then engage in the work of repair and care, regardless of what it costs relationally, emotionally, physically, and psychologically. Then he is on the path to becoming a man with character and integrity.

Choosing to Pick Up Our Cross

Right now, the world desperately needs men who are able to own and engage with the pain of their lives, the disappointments, and the brokenness, without blame and shame or pulling out the "victim card" to get sympathy when they really need to take responsibility. But men rarely get to this place in our culture because we're so busy making sure everyone is comfortable and feeling okay, never having to feel pain or feel inconvenienced at any time.

This is a massive issue. Too many times in the name of "compassion," we pull people (or ourselves) off the "cross" before they die. Yet we are told that we're supposed to be picking up our cross daily. That's the central reality of making Jesus our model for living and for manhood. He boldly told us, "'If anyone would come after me, let him deny himself and take up his cross daily and follow me. For whoever would save his life will lose it, but whoever loses his life for my sake will save it'" (Luke 9:23–24).

The cross is a picture of the rejection, pain, sacrifice, and suffering we must endure, even when we've done nothing wrong. You are "taking up your cross" to reveal who you were always meant to be, while engaging in the redemption of those you hurt and those who hurt you, even if they are the ones you love or the ones who claim to love you. We've been falsely taught that someone should come and save and rescue us from our painful circumstances, so we are hoping to *escape* rather than *engage* in our lives, in the story we have been given, as well as with the choices we have made. We want a way out without ever having to fully die.

The issue with doing this is twofold: first, we miss the redemptive power of sacrificial living, and second, we never have to engage with the ego-killing submission required to find our true identity. We cannot avoid sacrifice in our lives. Either we choose it, or life chooses it for us. Choosing to eat healthy instead of living off fast food is a sacrifice, but if you don't choose to make that sacrifice today, the health issues that potentially will arise in the future will demand sacrifices tomorrow, next week, or next year. We must learn to pay the price today for the future we hope for tomorrow, as well as learn to trust that God knows what He's doing.

So regardless of my understanding or the cost, I fully surrender to the story and life I've been given to fulfill God's purposes in me and through me. By doing so, I submit to His will, His purpose, and His plan, recognizing that nothing is wasted by our God, who still makes beauty from ashes. Submission to Him points me in the direction of who He knows I can become instead of just settling for what others expect of me.

Jesus answers both issues when He stands before Pilate in John 19. Pilate tells Jesus, "Don't you know I have the authority to have you killed?" And Jesus responds with, "You have no authority except that which was given to you by my Father in heaven" (my paraphrase of verses 10–11). Jesus' life was not taken from Him; it was a willing sacrifice from a man whose life was fully submitted to God. Because He knew who He was and why He had been sent, Jesus could consciously make that choice. No one murdered Him. He wasn't a doormat others were allowed to walk all over. He was participating wholeheartedly in His life and His part of the story as a willing servant sacrificing whatever was necessary—even His own life—for the sake of redemption, resurrection, and reconciliation.

As men (or women), we must stop helping people escape their circumstances, avoid their pain, and reject the story they are *actually* living. Helping someone avoid or detach from his (or her) experience is the strategy of the *enemy*, not the strategy of *heaven*. The enemy wants to offer you opportunities to fulfill your God-given potential without you ever having to die, without you ever having to suffer, and most assuredly without you making any sacrifice. This is what he offered Eve in the garden, what he offered Jesus in the desert, and what he offers us on a regular basis to limit our growth while keeping us in cycles of guilt and shame, in order to maintain control over our story. We have a very real enemy, and taking him up on his offers never helps us fulfill our potential. In fact, it does just the opposite.

When Jesus was at the end of His forty-day fast in the desert—when He was at His weakest point, but was also only moments away from His greatest breakthrough of returning to the city endued with power from on high—the enemy offered

32

Him three ways that He could fulfill His God-given potential without ever having to die (see Luke 4:1–13). The devil tempted Jesus to provide for Himself by turning stones into bread (provision), to bow before him to get back the authority Satan had gained in the garden of Eden (promotion), and to throw Himself off the temple to test God and have the angels rescue Him (protection). These same three offerings come to us regularly: temptations to gain for ourselves provision, promotion, and protection. They come in a thousand different ways, a thousand different times over the course of our lives, but they will always fall into the same categories Jesus faced in the desert:

1. Will you settle for provision—the money, the stuff, the temporary and fleeting things of the world that will go in and out of fashion and will fade, rust, and deteriorate? Or will you be satisfied and grateful with where you are and what you have?

2. Will you compromise just a little when no one is looking to receive the promotion that you believe you deserve, or that it was prophesied you would obtain, or that you know you were made for, in order to avoid the sacrifices and pain it would require to do it right over the next five or ten years? Or will you pursue promotion in a way that sustains your integrity and develops your character?

3. Will you give up or give in when someone or something offers to save you from the pain and offers protection and covering and reprieve from your experience? Or will you willingly engage in the moment you were given as a gift, regardless of the cost, and not attempt to avoid it or to simply "get over it"?

Your job is not to rescue, to fix, to figure out, or to make someone feel better. Your goal as a man is to make sure the person in front of you, starting with your own family, feels seen as you are able, with kindness and care, to bear witness to his or her experience. Remind the people around you daily, and in some seasons hour by hour, that their struggle does not go unnoticed. When your wife is hurting, sure, bring her flowers. But then engage with her pain. Sit with her in it. I don't care if it makes you uncomfortable.

If you have a friend who is losing everything, sit with that person in it, grab a coffee, and don't use phrases like "it's going to be okay." You don't know it will be okay. The only reason we say things like that is because we're uncomfortable and feel awkward about someone's circumstances, and in many ways we're probably avoiding our own. So to continue avoiding our struggles, we help others avoid theirs. This cycle will continue until one man decides he isn't going to run anymore, and he isn't going to let someone else run either. Jesus began this over two thousand years ago, and we can join Him in it today if we are willing to make Him our model of masculinity.

Now, let me make this clear before we move forward: There is a difference between the circumstantial, situational experiences I was just referring to and the violating, unjust acts that require men to step in and do something without concern for their personal well-being. While there are times when men need to know how to sit with others and provide care without attempting to rescue or fix things, there are also situations where a man needs to know how to take a punch or give one, utilizing discernment to know how and when to protect and defend those who are being mistreated or are in danger. Men need to know how to sit with the suffering, but they also need to be able to stand aggressively against a violent man attempting to attack their family. A man needs to be able to weep with those whose hearts are broken, but then turn around and use that same strength to run inside a burning building to save a small child.

An Invitation to Come, Die, and Live

We must develop a masculinity that can humble itself before the throne of Jesus, while opposing wicked systems and structures that oppose the basic human rights of others. This requires wisdom, training, mentorship, physical and emotional strength, confidence, identity—all the things we will continue to explore with each pathway we journey down in this book.

But this journey toward masculinity is not a demand.

Everything I have just described to you is an invitation.

An invitation away from the false gospel of this age that bids us to "come and live, so that you will never have to die." An invitation into the true Gospel of Jesus Christ that calls us to "come and die, so that you might live."

Yet sadly, based on studies about the absence of male role models and data on the struggles today's young men face, most men will never venture down these pathways. They will avoid, deflect, justify, and remain stagnant where they are. Their stories will remain untold, their marriages unchanged, and their children uninspired, and we will all be lesser for it.

We need one another, if this is going to change.

THE WORK

The end of each chapter will include what we will call "The Work." You will find steps to take along each specific path to help you move forward on your journey. Our first tools are a notebook or journal and a pen—something to record your journey and your progress as you process all that you experience along the way.

These are the first among the many tools I will offer you in this book for the journey ahead. But let me make it clear that these first two are not optional tools if you decide to move forward. Truly, they have more value than I can express in a few simple pages.

We have books and studies over the past fifty-plus years that show the physical, psychological, emotional, and spiritual implications of simply writing. Such an exercise is what author and artist Julia Cameron calls "Morning Pages," and what professor and psychologist James W. Pennebaker, PhD, calls "Expressive Writing." For our use here, we'll call it "Morning + Evening Notes." You miss a day, a week, whatever, no big deal. Just start again, and keep writing. This isn't about whether you like it or get it or hate your handwriting or don't want people to read it. This is about health, strength, and connecting with yourself and your story in ways you may never have done before. I recommend getting a nice notebook and a good pen, something of value that carries with it the seriousness of your intention.

But what do I write down?

It's easier than you think, but more difficult than you might assume.

The goal as we begin is to write two times a day, morning notes and evening notes. Let's look at each.

Morning notes. Morning notes are for writing *what you're currently feeling and why*. Whatever is bothering you, stressing you, frustrating you—write it all down, even if all you write is "I hate Jake Hamilton and the fact that I have to do this. It's stupid and has no value."

That's a great first step toward engaging what's happening inside you with honesty and vulnerability. What happened the day before? Process it on the page, with raw emotion. You say you don't know what emotion you're feeling because that's completely new to you? We've got you covered there too. Just turn to the "Emotions and Sensations List" provided in appendix IV, choose three words from three different categories, and start there. You've probably never been asked to do this before, so don't beat yourself up while you are learning and referencing the list. You don't need to add shame and guilt to the equation.

Then here's the rough part: *Write down one "secret" about your life and your story.* It can be recent, it can be from your childhood, or it can be anywhere in between; it just has to be true. No need at this point to write out the full story in detail; just a simple few lines will do. I'm not looking for you to write only the secrets that are traumatic or marking, although that's part of it. I'm also asking you to *write down the secrets about who you are and what you long for. What is it that you dream about or imagine?* If you've lost that ability, today you can re-kindle it by asking yourself, *What did I imagine or daydream about when I was a child?*

Don't try to make your morning notes longer than they need to be or more perfect than I'm asking for. Just a few lines, maybe five to ten minutes to start, can change your life.

Evening notes. And now the evening notes, which are for writing down *what you are grateful for* each night before your head hits the pillow. Again, this may sound simple, but if you've had a frustrating or stress-filled day, it may be a real challenge to find three to five things you're grateful for. But that's the work. Gratefulness is a key ingredient of resiliency in your own identity and in relationships. There is never a time when it's "all bad." There is always something you can find to say thank you for when you're looking.

But why are we doing this?

We are doing this exercise to get what's inside us—in our hearts, in our heads, circling around in irrational thought patterns—outside us, onto a piece of paper where we can look at these things and better evaluate them so they don't express themselves in explosive or reclusive behaviors. Once a thought has passed through your heart, into your mind, out of your hands, and before your eyes, these filters will allow you to see it and explore it in ways you may never have done before. This may lead you to new conclusions you have never found before.

The goal is exploration. Through your "Morning + Evening Notes," you are building a backward map from where you have been, to bear witness at an undetermined date in the future to how far you have come.

So before you continue with this book, buy yourself something to write in or staple some paper together, get a nice pen or a felt-tip marker, and start writing. You're not just plotting a course back home; you're building a road map for your great-grandchildren.

See you in the next chapter, on the next path, as we step into a bigger story.

Path 2

Stepping into a Bigger Story

> By going deeper into myth, I go deeper into love, and when
> I go deeper into love, innately I find morality; I locate a True
> North in my own heart.
>
> —Martin Shaw

It was a long drive from where we were living in Southern California to our two nights away in Las Vegas for our anniversary, where we would watch a couple of shows and get a nice dinner. Nicci and I had just worked through a major crisis in our marriage, after I had finished leading worship in one of the largest gatherings I had ever been invited to participate in. There was no infidelity, no addiction, no abuse. There was just a minister, a worship leader, traveling too much in the name of a "calling," pursuing what I felt the Lord had said, but running over my family in the process and being on the road too much. The cost had finally taken a toll on my marriage. The day after I had been at this huge event in Chicago, as we sat with a trusted mentor, my wife poured out her heart and her pain in a way

I had never seen before. She said she wasn't leaving, although she wanted to, but she couldn't pretend anymore. She couldn't keep feeling this abandonment and rejection and pretend it was okay.

It was only about four weeks after this experience in Chicago, and we were back on speaking terms through a series of events I won't get into right now, for the sake of time and space. Although things weren't fixed, we had begun on the road to healing. I was in counseling, attempting to understand the brokenness in my own story while trying to make space to understand the brokenness in my wife's story. And here was the moment when it began to click. As we were speeding along the 15 freeway from California to Nevada, I began to ask my wife the most random questions about her childhood. I realized that I didn't know this woman and her life the way I thought I did, and I needed to understand her story, her heart, in new ways if we were ever going to grow from this.

My questions didn't begin as deep, meaningful, or even significant; they were just about what shows she had watched, what games she had played, what Christmas gifts were her favorite. Then from those simple questions, they grew into connected and curious questions about what it was like with her mom growing up, what it was like to have no dad in the home, her dating experience, her friends when she was young, what she had dreamed about when she was four. The questions just went on and on from the drive there, all throughout the weekend. By the time we arrived home, we were in such deep conversation that we sat in the car for another couple of hours. It clicked for me that my traveling, my life, was hurting Nicci because my story of significance was smashing into her story of trauma, and both of us were missing an opportunity to bring healing to one another because we had never taken the time to explore each other's stories. We had never asked deep and thoughtful questions and genuinely listened to each other about how our childhood experiences have shaped us into the people we are today.

All of our stories—the experiences we have had from the ages of two to twenty—have made us who we are today and deserve to be heard, witnessed, and held in a safe and loving space so we can know the feeling of security and containment. My wife and I began to do this for each other on a regular basis every time we felt anxiety or frustration or rejection, you name it. The value of personal story within connected relationships has been solidified in such a significant way that we can't go back.

The Mythic Side of the Story

That's the personal side of the story. But what about the mythic side? What about the parables, the fairy tales, the stories that come from cultures and tribes that explore and expand the space beyond our personal stories? What about the space of the imagination, and the symbols that invite us to see what we could not see through simple informative facts about subjects and situations in our life? (As we start down this path, by the way, it will be helpful to note that I will use the words *myth*, *story*, and *parable* interchangeably throughout this book.)

I will never forget the first time I read the Grimm fairy tale "Iron John," the story of a young prince and a giant of a man covered in red hair from head to toe. This giant was found alive, wrapped in a cloth and shivering at the bottom of a pond. He would carry the boy prince into initiation, manhood, and the adventure of a lifetime. The full story (which I encourage you to read) follows the young boy's journey from the palace to the wilderness, to the work force, to love, to the battlefield, and finally into the arms of his bride. His journey has come to define symbolically what it means to become a man. "Iron John" has been used to chart the male experience through initiation for decades now, but it took on new recognition in 1990, when the incredible author, poet, and men's movement leader Robert Bly released his book *Iron John: A Book about Men*.

At that point in my life, I wasn't interested in fantastic tales. I had been in ministry for almost two decades, and I didn't need myth; I needed facts. I needed linear, concrete information about what passages, what tools, what information would keep my kids from sin, my family healthy, and my heart thriving in God.

This is the environment we now live in when we enter the Church. Gone is the world of awe and wonder and mystery and tension and conflicting ideas. In its place are systematic theology, dogma, and rhetoric, all in the name of keeping us "safe" from the enemy and his schemes. Sometimes I think we are more afraid of the devil than we are in awe of God. Our language demands "repeat after me" discipleship programs, "work harder" evangelism strategies, and "romantic songs" to Jesus that could just as easily be country radio hits. Now, I agree that we need theology, we need evangelism, we need discipleship. Obviously, I sing songs about the love of Jesus. Yet the bridge between organizational realities that offer us the appearance of safety, and the overwhelming and indescribable reality of a living God who is both death and resurrection, the Lion and the Lamb, is the world of myth and parable.

The mythological realm of storytelling gives us a frame of reference for our personal experience, without the consequences of shame and guilt. We can see and accept truths that we would oppose if they were simply given to us at face value. This mythic realm allows each person to see the same story from a different angle, based on his or her circumstances and experiences. The purpose of story—whether Odysseus's great journeys in

Homer's *The Iliad* and *The Odyssey*, or Jesus' stories of the lost coin or the sower who sows seed—is that it becomes a simple and beautiful way of revealing deeper truths in a way that the common man can engage with. No degrees are necessary, and all ages from five to one hundred can understand it.

Martin Shaw says, "Myth is our wild way of telling the truth."[1] I love that sense of wildness that is revealed when we go back to telling the stories. If we would take the stories of Jesus out of the cages of doctrine we've confined them to and let them out in the surrounding world again, what would happen? What if men were just able to share freely with their families story after story, inspiring awe, reading old classics and giving our children a chance to be children again, with vivid imaginations not weighed down by the screens we chain the kids to for our convenience?

The Eternal Side of the Story

This connection between our personal story and the mythological or parabolic world allows us to enter into the third realm of story with eyes wide open, with hope and expectations. Beyond personal stories and mythic stories, this third realm is the eternal story—the story of God throughout all of time, connecting all of creation and all of humanity in a sacred bond to His heart. In the Church, we've been asking the question "What does it mean?" about this third realm for so long that we have forgotten to connect with the real question, which is "What does it reveal?" We keep searching the eternal story of God, the living and written Word, for all traces of system and structure, when the whole time it has been revealing a Man, not a method.

This doesn't often provide us with the comfort we're looking for. When we struggle with concepts too large for us to grasp or pain too deep for us to express, Jesus offers us awe instead of answers, and then He points us to greater depths of beauty and mystery. The real beauty of engaging consistently with our personal story and exploring ancient and medieval myths is that it opens our eyes to the possibilities of what God's eternal story could potentially be pointing us to. Since I've already quoted Martin Shaw more than once, let's do it again. He puts it like this: "Myth told me everything I needed to know about the conditions of life. Christianity [*Jesus*] showed me how to live it."[2]

This is a dangerous revelation because if it points to a Person, a Being so profound, so dynamic, and so powerful that this story cannot be contained in one expression or perspective, then we lose our ability to control the story—where it goes, what it looks like, and whom it encounters. Our responsibility as Bible-believing men is not to develop greater theological understanding (although there is a place for that), but to take ownership of the life we were given and tell the eternal story. Your family, your wife and kids, your friends won't encounter God because of a good theological argument; they will encounter Him because you're willing to share your encounter vulnerably and courageously with them. This doesn't happen overnight; this is a lifestyle. It's masculinity lived out over a lifetime as we explore these three areas of story: the personal, the mythological, and the eternal.

These three types of story dance with and reveal one another. Myth comes from our personal story encountering the eternal story in a language that makes sense to us and to others in our culture. The eternal story gives context to our personal story and is then shared through mythological lenses to help others understand the complexity and beauty of it. Think about it historically. Men would gather around campfires and tell eternal stories long before anything was ever written down and generations before anything became known as "the canon of Scripture."

Can you imagine the first time the stories you now hold in your Bible were told around campfires and dinner tables, and then passed along orally? The excitement, the energy, as people heard about who God was and what He did? From Abraham to David, to the kings of old, to Jesus Himself, these stories were shared with friends and family in common places. Way before Scriptures were debated in cathedrals and divided up over denominational lines, these stories were passionately portrayed through fathers to sons and daughters in poetic narrative around the family table. Even forty days after the resurrection, Jesus went through the whole story of the Scriptures and showed His followers He was there all along, revealing Himself, revealing the Spirit, while they were busy setting up new laws from old doctrines. This is the power of story. It allows us to see the heart of the matter in the context of a bigger picture.

This is what makes Scripture accessible. Yet we have made men feel stupid by convincing generations of them that officially sanctioned theological rhetoric is the only way to share Scripture with authority. So in fear of doing it wrong, men never share it at all, when in reality they could simply have been sitting around the fire and retelling the stories from memory, orally, with nuance and perspective, missing a few beats here and there, perhaps not remembering the names of Noah's sons, but telling the epic tale of God's flood with a heart to expose those who listened to a story bigger than themselves.

Or maybe it's a common story. It's "Iron John," it's "The Green Knight," it's "King Arthur and the Knights of the Round Table." It's folklore and fairy tale used to reveal something bigger to us, something behind the scenes, hidden in the recesses of our imagination. I promise you that this is what men are looking for in the Church.

Illustration or Illumination?

Maybe I'm wrong, and I apologize in advance if I take it too far, but I believe men need a space that trusts them and allows them to explore and decide things for themselves. We don't always have to agree in order to stay in community together. I don't want to be told what to think or be convinced that I don't understand, for the sake of control. Story takes off the restraints and allows us to engage with the process of transformation through language that draws me into places in my own heart I didn't even know I needed to visit. I believe that's why many men default to guns, because they are still looking for dragons to slay. Since we have removed that kind of language and imagination, they're finding dragons that aren't really there. They're creating their own dragons in their lives because they long for something to fight for and something to wrestle with in the midst of a community of men.

The problem isn't that we're more selfish or more broken than the previous generations. Sin is sin, and has been from the beginning. The truth is that we've become a people who have given up on the mythological in exchange for the literal, the logical, and the theological. We have left our imaginations at the door, and have since lost our ability to live in mystery and tension. We pretend to understand things as profound and complex as the Creation story, the incarnation, the atonement, and Communion, let alone salvation and redemption. We attempt with vanity to claim, *We have it figured out, we understand, so just follow me, because everyone else has it wrong.* . . . There are no differing perspectives allowed to live in the same room; it's either black or white, right or wrong, left or right.

Yet myth, story, and parable allow space for all of it as we pursue the same end, Christ and Christ alone. Even the great scholar and author Joseph Campbell, born a Catholic, immersed in his childhood in Christian imagery and story, is known to have said that all of his study and research was given a head start through his experience in the Church. But we must also say that he didn't follow through with his faith throughout the rest of his life because he became so disillusioned with a Church that had lost its divine imagination.

Once, the Church was a world full of images and substance that captivated and awed those who entered. But we gave it all up for pragmatism and dogmatism, which have only further separated and alienated us from one another. Most men are leaving the institutionalized Church because it has left them wanting for more. We must rediscover the world of myth and nature and tradition that finds its center around the family table rather than the boardroom. We need a language that is bigger than the pulpit and goes beyond any single doctrine we might attempt to define. If that makes you uncomfortable, then we are heading in the right direction. Myth has a greater concern than being right. It longs to *reveal*.

This is the model of Jesus. He challenged religious norms through powerful parables, opting for illumination over illustration. Illustration is what we normally experience from the pulpit. It produces a single story, usually based in real life, possibly even in a testimony, that only points in one direction and leaves no room for the listeners' interpretation. This model usually stems from the fear that people won't understand, and the belief that if they do attempt to interpret a story for themselves, they'll get it wrong and not live the way God intends. Therefore, instead of freedom, we can only offer control, or worse, manipulation, from our stories. That's no longer parable; that's propaganda.

Illumination, on the other hand, gives us a story bigger than real life, often with characters and symbolism that pull us out of our reality and into someplace new. Think of *The Chronicles of Narnia, The Lord of the Rings,* and so many other stories that give plenty of opportunity for the listeners to decide for themselves what each symbol means and what each character represents, depending on where they are personally and what they've experienced in their own journey. The storyteller trusts that the Spirit of God will lead people into truth, not our communication or the parts of the story we emphasized or forgot.

Look at the story of the Good Samaritan, as told by Jesus in Luke 10:25–37. First, it's a "fake story," possibly arising from cultural norms, but still made up. It never actually happened. Not one theologian I have studied actually believed that the parables were real events from Jesus' life; the consensus is that He simply made them up to point to a greater truth. So they are all likely "once upon a time" stories. *Parable* literally means "fictitious story."[3] I love that. Then, the story itself relates a highly unlikely set of circumstances that probably would never have happened. It's a myth in the best sense of the word, giving us people grounded in real life, in a world we understand, with impossible circumstances that eventually point us to a greater truth than we would ever experience in our everyday life. There are so many options for us to explore as we hear it. We don't have to feel bad for being the characters who passed by the injured man; we live it through the story and are able to recognize that tendency within ourselves.

And Jesus doesn't follow this story up with a dissertation about the points. He leaves. Myth forces us to release control, to be surprised, and to engage in new ways with the faith we hold so dear. That's what happened with the Pharisees listening to Jesus in that moment. They knew who they were in the story, but they had to bear the weight of what it meant. Jesus called them out and showed all of us how to love our neighbor. That's the power of myth. When we hear a story like this, larger than ourselves, we will be found either attempting in futility to figure out what it means, or simply yielding to the mystery of what we've just heard and allowing it to change us and challenge us at the same time.

Engage with and Embrace Your Story

As we continue our exploration together, we will follow the mythological story of "Parzival and the Quest for the Holy Grail" as a framework to illuminate the power of biblical masculinity. I am not the first to use Parzival in this way, and I know I won't be the last. It has been done by men of great intellect and experience for decades. Carl Jung, Joseph Campbell, Robert A. Johnson, Father Richard Rohr, Martin Shaw, and many others have explored this text for the psychological, mythological, and yes, even spiritual implications it makes. I recognize that what I'm attempting to offer here is a slight deviation from what they attempted to cover. Yet I hope that I'm also building upon what they so powerfully invested into the work of this story. My hope is to allow you, the listener, the reader, to engage with the story, the study, and the work in such a way that you are able to find your identity and destiny unfolding in front of you as we journey together.

This is about your story encountering the mythological story of Parzival, to reveal your story and the eternal story of God. This journey won't require a doctorate in divinity to understand it. It will pull you from a safe, rationalized, theologically driven relationship with God into something more profound and powerful than you could ever have imagined. The modern-day attempt to rationalize all aspects of our faith has led today's men to believe that they cannot lead their families into a deep and meaningful relationship with God. But you can, and you absolutely will. You can learn to tell stories as you learn the value of your own story. In your own unique way, you will learn to share your heart, ask questions that matter, and call people into the fullness of all they were created for.

When we engage with story in this way, we find that we don't simply tell a story; the story tells us. We see things in ourselves that we passed over or avoided because we weren't invited into them by our caregivers, or we were never taught to use the tools to engage with them within ourselves. As you read and engage with the story of Parzival, you will find that the places in you that were "fine" will slowly be excavated to reveal the hidden pain and brokenness inside—not to shame you, but to reveal you to yourself.

This was the foundation beneath all great myth and all the great initiation rites for young men throughout history. Boys were prepared and encouraged over the course of their youth to look at their weakness, intentionally engage with it, overcome it, and find strength in it. This process would culminate in some type of ceremony or task where a young man would go out into the wilderness alone to forge weapons, endure pain, hunt, and fight. He would then return to the tribe or community with a wound, a marking, from the experience. To be appropriately "wounded" in some way that had purpose and meaning gave young men the ability to look back at what they had endured with hope and a sense of *"I can make it through anything."*

The myth reveals the life, and the life reveals the myth. If you were able to encounter mythological stories repeatedly at a young age, connected to rites of passage, then they became tools in your belt to help you recognize purpose in the midst of your struggles and limitations. Every time you encountered pain, suffering, heartbreak, or loss, you would be able to rise up to the occasion because you knew it had a purpose. Every time you were wounded, you wouldn't become offended or play the victim. You would turn your pain, rejection, emotional scars, and the physical and emotional suffering you had endured into sacred wounds that you would proudly show off. These wounds could be everything from when you were made fun of at school, to the abuse you suffered, to the abandonment you endured, all of which have shaped you into becoming the man you are today. Myth gave you context for your experience, and initiation gave it the practical application.

Your sacred wounds, the myths, and the initiatory experience were all showing you that anything is possible. The goal of young men engaging in rites of passage is that one day, when you find yourself amid another setback or defeat, you can recall this wounding, these stories, your experience, and pull it into your current circumstance to find the faith, courage, and confidence to move forward despite how things might appear.

Mature masculinity doesn't avoid the wound, the pain, the sacrifice, the suffering. It celebrates them. It thanks God for them. It's not masochistic in nature, making things hard when they don't have to be, in the name of "growth." Mature men appropriately choose the harder path because they can see it for what it is, an opportunity. They don't cry and complain about it when it comes; they don't give up or give in. They don't default to addictions and abandon their families. Men who have been initiated and have matured use their pain to pursue their promise. They believe their life is anchored to a story bigger than the one they are currently experiencing.

Engaging with your personal story and embracing it are the first steps toward male initiation. Ownership leads to responsibility. Where you have been will reveal where you are going, because there is no arriving; there is only going forward. Your future is completely dependent on how you view your past. Successes and failures are simply signposts along your unique pathway as you continue on your journey. All of it belongs because God wastes nothing. I love the way professor and psychiatrist Irvin Yalom put it, quoting Thomas Hardy: "If a way to the Better there be, it exacts a full look at the Worst."[4] That's what makes this work so difficult. We cannot simply look at all our positive attributes and outcomes and think we can live fully alive in who we were meant to be. We have to step into a bigger story and then engage with and embrace our own.

THE WORK

Before you move on to the next path, let me ask you a few questions to further the work as you respond to this chapter. Remember to open your notebook and write down your answers so you can chart your progress and your exploration.

1. Have you ever looked at your story before? If so, what has that process been like for you? If not, why not?

2. What is your first memory? When you look back as far as you can, what do you find? Was there love, pain, sadness, fear? Just write down whatever memory is there, and a few details from it. What does that memory make you feel today?

3. What fairy tales, mythological stories, or even bedtime stories do you remember from your childhood? What story stands out? What about the story do you remember? What emotions come up as you reflect on that story now?

4. What stories do you enjoy today (from books, movies, or other media)? What type of stories are you drawn to, and why? What about these stories speaks to you? It might just be for entertainment, but is there something else? What do you observe about the themes you engage with?

Path 3

Embracing Where You Came From

> Our story gives a teaching diametrically opposite. It says
> that where a man's wound is, that is where his genius will be.
>
> —Robert Bly, *Iron John: A Book about Men*

The version of "Parzival and the Quest for the Holy Grail" that I will share with you is my interpretation of the story. As I mentioned in the introduction, this is only possible because of Martin Shaw's tremendous work, whose version was the first one I found in simple narrative form. As I also mentioned, I couldn't have done this without the twenty-four thousand lines of the story translated into English by Zeydel and Morgan. I have made the story my own, emphasizing what I felt necessary for the sake of our purposes here and using it as a framework for the journey into masculinity.

With that being said, the story of Parzival begins much like your story, with one family, broken and beautiful and with complexities our young hero won't discover until he is busy tripping over them. And therein lies the difficulty—you don't get to pick the family you were born into or the lineage you inherited. You walked into the middle of a story, not the beginning. As did Parzival, whose story I'll begin here:

With Parzival the opening scene focuses on the mother, the White Queen, Herzeloyde (which means "Heart-Sorrow"), who was longing for a husband. She had lived in her tower alone, her beauty beyond compare, and her rule as kind and steadfast as there had ever been or ever would be. Her subjects loved and adored her, and many a man had attempted to win her hand, but could not. So in an attempt to find someone her heart would leap for, she threw a tournament.

Men came from every corner of the earth to win the hand of the White Queen. Many of them had attempted before to no avail, but they came again, hoping their fortunes would change. Yet all other knights found it hard to shine while resting in the shadow of the Dark Knight from the East, Gahmuret, who stood head and shoulders above the rest. They say that men of all faiths and all backgrounds held him in such high esteem that none, not even Arthur's father, Uther Pendragon himself, could catch the attention of the White Queen after he came on the scene.

The Dark Knight's voice carried the weight of his experience. His skin was a deep olive, tattooed with scars from the battles he had won. His hair was as black as the night sky itself. His sword thundered with each blow he delivered. He could tame the wildest of stallions. Yet his poetic language and insight made even the most vibrant lilies blush, and he was well-versed in history and prose. Gahmuret, the Dark Knight of the East, won Herzeloyde's heart, and she eagerly married him and gave him her virginity.

And in the beginning, there was bliss.

But the rumors soon followed. Rumors that Gahmuret was already married to the Black Queen, Belacane, and that he was father to a young boy with splotched skin, black and white like a magpie.

54

The White Queen ignored all these rumors and persisted in her love, but the bliss they had known for such a short time now rode on choppy waters.

▼ ▼ ▼

We must immediately address that this story about the masculine journey begins with the feminine. Like every man, the time we spent in our mother's womb attuned us to the frequency of the feminine before we were ever introduced to the acceptance of a father. We hoped in our small, frail bodies that the outer world would give us much of what we experienced in the womb—a mother who covered, cared for, and nurtured us, and a father who protected and provided so she could do so. But as we know ourselves and will see in Parzival's story, this is not usually the case.

The White Queen wasn't a tame, subjugated feminine figure in our story, but was a woman who, in her loneliness and sorrow, didn't leave her fate up to chance. She grasped the reins of her life and boldly set the stage for her own future. Herzeloyde is a powerful and dynamic figure, especially when you think of this story being told in the time it came from. She didn't wait for squired knights and princes to come her way led by her family or father. She knew who she was and the value of her place in the world, and she took action.

Although Herzeloyde was sorrowful in her heart, she was quite the opposite in her actions. This is something for us to see and understand as the story unfolds. The White Queen knew what she wanted her life to look like and wasn't afraid to take the proper steps to see it happen. Many women like this in our culture are looked down upon, called names, and pushed aside, especially in the Church. But just because a woman is powerful and decisive, she shouldn't be labeled a Jezebel. Queen Herzeloyde longed to be married, serve a husband, build a home, and become a mother. She wanted to direct all that courage and confidence into people she loved. We cannot misjudge or misdiagnose powerful women in our culture because they expose our insecurities. Powerful women don't cause men to be weak; they expose the weakness already there.

No Perfect Past Stories

Men like Gahmuret should rise to occasion and stand above their peers as they walk out into life with courage and confidence, not arrogance and ego. Yet our story reveals that the Dark Knight had been humbled by life before he ever arrived on the battlefield. His experiences, failures, and victories had shaped him into the man he was, but much of what he had experienced was unresolved and undealt with. When we refuse to engage with that which has formed us, our cracks are eventually revealed. The mystery of Gahmuret was quickly exposed by the rumors that flew around the couple. Even strong men have past stories they don't want to deal with. They simply decide that the best option is to move forward, and that everyone they leave behind would be better off without them. So they run from battle to battle, war to war, thinking they can build a better story by ignoring the one they left. But the truth is that you cannot build a house on a faulty foundation.

And don't you dare think your family is any different.

There are no perfect parents. There are no perfect homes, perfect lives, perfect families—none, not one. Let the myth of perfection dissipate like the mist and vapor that it is. If you need to hold together some perfect image of your parents or your upbringing, then you're doing that for you. It's there to protect something in you that you don't want to deal with, but one day you'll have to. Maybe it will be when you have kids, when your marriage isn't going the way you hoped, or when you lose the security you're so desperately clinging to.

This is where I lose so many men in coaching and in preaching, because they feel as if it's their job to protect their parents. Something deep and primal rises up in them and wants to tell me, "Stop! My parents did the best they could." That alone is a terrible place to be as a son because you're not supposed to be your parents' defenders; they're supposed to be yours. So we are already in a difficult place emotionally, psychologically, and of course spiritually. Most men I work with think their only option is to make their parents bad or good, which isn't the case at all. The work of engaging with your childhood and your story isn't about deciding where to place blame or who was "bad" and who was "good." It's about exposing the story you're telling yourself and how that differs from the story you actually lived.

The beauty of knowing and owning your story is that it empowers you to identify your wounds, where they came from, and how they impact the life you are living today. Your story began before you were born, with beautifully broken individuals who attempted to bring you up in the pain and promises they still carried. Some parents resorted to violence and control, manipulation and deceit, while others resorted to spoiling, giving their kids whatever they wanted whenever they wanted it. Some parents sheltered their kids from the world, wrapping them in a bubble of safety and religion so they wouldn't be exposed to culture, music, television, and more. These parents hoped their kids wouldn't experience any harm, but mostly hoped they themselves wouldn't experience any harm either.

I know these are overexaggerations in both directions. And if you suffered severe abuse in your childhood, just be aware that we won't be discussing that topic at length. It deserves specialized attention and care from professionals who know how to walk you into healing and wholeness. My level of competency simply cannot provide that through a few pages in a book. What I'm referring to in our discussion are the thousands of shades of experience that happen in between these extremes, experiences that define most of humanity's childhood homes. We must gain tools and do what I call the "work" of going back into those wounds and finding the men God intended us to be, despite how off course we might currently be. This brings up the next issue we have: the lack of fatherhood in a culture desperately longing for a king.

▼ ▼ ▼

After many months, Gahmuret heard there were invaders in the land of his birth. A war had broken out there, and he desired to be of assistance. It was the sound of his old life, his comrades, his purpose calling him, and he had to answer. There was no remorse in this; it was simply a fact of life, who he was, and the man Herzeloyde had married.

As he left, his wife's belly was growing. The child they had conceived was a reminder of the reunion she so desperately longed for. She grasped tightly to her husband's promise to return to her, but as she would soon learn, it was a promise he could not keep. The news of Gahmuret's death was mourned by all. Even his enemies gathered to mourn him and celebrate his life. Some say that the war he went to fight ceased that day because so many wanted to honor this warrior and brother.

But it was too much for the White Queen who was left behind. Herzeloyde became inconsolable, and it was in that grief, in that dark, lonely despair, that she gave birth to a son, Parzival. And on that day, she swore an oath that he would know nothing of his father, that he would *not* grow up in the world of posturing and falsehoods that had taken her husband's life. She took Parzival to the edge of the forest to live with her there, where he would know nothing of quests and battles. In fact, he grew up not even knowing his own name. He was simply called

Dear Boy or Beautiful Son, and because of those declarations spoken over him daily, he came to know something of his inner glory. This is usually given to young boys by the feminine side of their world, but he was denied approval or verification of that glory, which can only come from the masculine in the outer world.

This is the context for the upbringing of Parzival, son of Gahmuret—a fatherless environment where the feminine covered and corralled his masculine longings in poverty and loneliness, where all who knew who he was were forbidden to speak of it around him. His mother, once the White Queen, the jewel of the kingdom, spoke only of religious life and limited landscapes. She taught him devotion to the Scriptures, and of the spiritual realm's duality—angels and demons, good and evil, right and wrong. Nothing of mystery and tension, commitment and magic, romance, and devotion to a cause. He grew into a young man knowing only the grief of his mother and the beauty of the emerald fields that surrounded him. But that much grief and limit is not good for a boy.

▼ ▼ ▼

Fathers have been in decline globally for a long time now. Instead of a position of honor and dignity at home and in society, they are now the punch line of every joke and the court jesters on our television screens. The war on patriarchal abuses became an assault on traditional masculinity, and eventually on men in general. Men are almost completely absent as educators. There are fewer male teachers in schools, and even fewer going to college to become educators. That means in the foreseeable future, young boys attending school could be entering a nearly all-female environment for twelve years. Then they will go home to an all-female environment where their fathers are not present.[1] Men have been pushed to the fringes of society, put down, and swept aside, and nobody is fighting to welcome them back because we can't see the value of the traditional roles that have sustained culture for hundreds of years.

59

When people don't feel valued, whether male or female, they recoil and regress into their base desires. They attempt to find a place where they are celebrated and their needs for affirmation and affection are met. If the water always runs to the lowest place, then men slide down that slope into addiction, depression, violence, and everything in between. Even hyper-religious behavior, although more tolerated in church circles, isn't a sign of devotion, but in most cases is a cover-up for needs not being met elsewhere.

I'm not making excuses for men. There are hundreds of ways they need to be displaying manhood more courageously. But I am asking all of us to pay attention to the current cultural climate and learn to fight for masculinity in a way that honors God, respects women, and protects children at all costs. I stated earlier that it's not strong women who make weak men. It's insecure men who abdicate their roles to strong women instead of partnering with them to accomplish something they could never accomplish on their own. We are to be dance partners, leaning into one another in an act of mutual submission, where the strengths of one prop up the weaknesses of the other as we live together for the greater good of our families, not for the individual gain of one of us over the other.

The Effects of a "Father Wound"

When we fail to see these realities in our culture and our homes, we miss the value of fathers being in the house daily with their children, in support of their wives. We tend to think it's optional for children to have a dad present. It's not. Children need to see their father committed to their mother and making the appropriate sacrifices for his family, regardless of what he gains in the process. You cannot be a dad 50 percent of the time and expect 100 percent positive results. This dad deficit in the home has led to young boys who don't know who they are and who can't compete in the educational or occupational realms. They give up before they get started, because a man hasn't stepped in and called them to step up.

A mother is the one in the home who says, "I love you! You're beautiful!" Even when you burn down the house, she says, "Isn't he so cute? He was attempting to camp in the living room." In this way, she provides the context for unconditional love for her boy, where he knows he has an inner value that cannot be swayed by better performance. This sets a boy up to encounter the first man in his life, his father. A father doesn't have to choose the boy, receive the boy, love the boy. Yet when he does, it's an invitation into the masculine realm that marks the boy for life. If the mother's love is the love that is truly unconditional, then the father's love is the love that first lets the boy know he is chosen.

When you remove being chosen from the equation, you have a boy who knows he has value, but doesn't know where to invest that value. So he constantly needs women to cater to him and serve him in his needs, his emotions, his life. Then when the women in his life don't cater to him, he feels something is wrong with them, not him. To his mother, he is Dear Boy and Beautiful Son, so he believes every woman he encounters should feel the same way about him, serve him, and make the whole world about him. You then end up with a boy (or adult man) who is so desperate for feminine affirmation that he is unable to fully embrace the world of the masculine with courage and confidence. Boys need fathers who temper the love and value lavished on them by their mothers in childhood into something powerful as they grow that will help a young man fully engage with the world he inhabits.

But like Parzival in our story, when a young man doesn't have that present father, a "father wound" is formed. Studies show that 33 percent of children in America, or 24.7 million kids, go home to a residence without a biological father present.[2] That's one-third of all our children! Likewise, fatherlessness is a huge issue in many other countries around the world. The absence of a father in the home does more than just make a young boy feel as though he is not chosen. It also allows all the negative voices in his life to determine for him what he is worth in the world. This is because no father was standing next to him, training and equipping him to combat the voices of the bullies, the jealous, the frustrated, and the embittered he will encounter along his journey. His "father wound" therefore becomes the space in which the lies can enter about the value (or lack of it) he has on earth. There is no powerful masculine voice within him that can combat the voice of a teacher who tells him he is stupid, or a kid at school who calls him names.

There is also no training to do the practical things a traditional man often does. When something breaks in his home or on his car, the man with a father wound feels lost and aggravated. He often will think he's dumb and incapable of solving life's challenges, but the frustration isn't really at the task. It's at the father who never taught him how, who never cared enough to train and equip him for the life he would live.

This father wound manifests in a man's identity, sexuality, and spirituality by causing chaos in his heart through a lack of confidence in his own body, soul, and mind. So a wounded man attempts to prove his worth everywhere he goes, looking for male validation, for someone to see and affirm him. All the while, he dominates women, whether in public through serial dating and sexual exploits or in private through porn addiction. These are his attempts to find comfort by escaping his reality. Then when he finds a woman he wants to spend the rest of his life with, he finds it extremely difficult to talk about his feelings or be vulnerable. This creates a lack of intimacy in his relationships. These cycles, and so many more, continue throughout a man's life as he attempts to grow and connect and be known by others even though no father ever showed him how.

This isn't just about the father being gone either. This is about the father who comes home every day and is so beaten down by his own life, his own experience and inadequacies, his own shame and guilt that he has nothing left for his son but his "temperament, and not his teaching," as Robert Bly writes in *Iron John*.[3] All the son sees is the father's anger, frustration, addiction, and depression. The son never gets to see a day full of dead-end jobs, abusive bosses, unpaid bills, and a thousand other stressors that consume his father.

It didn't used to be that way. Before the white-collar work so many fathers do today away from home, where their young boys cannot see them, there were farms and blue-collar jobs sons could see. Boys could see a father's calloused hands, the sweat on his brow, the building that went up, the crop that was yielded, and they could admire and respect it. A young boy needs this, because he is born with a crown too big for his head, and he needs another man to hold it for him, to steward it until he is ready to wear it on his own. The "crown" represents who he truly is, who he was meant to be, his divine potential, and his unique destiny that was forged in eternity. This is the beautiful and complex role of the father that so many young boys are missing today, even if their biological father is still in the house. They need an engaged dad who is willing to do the work necessary to lead his sons from boyhood to manhood— something that was probably never done for him.

Turning Your Heart toward Home

If this was never done for you, where do you begin such a momentous feat, with absolutely no training and no time to learn?

You begin with Malachi 4:6, where the hearts of the fathers turn toward their children.

That's it. It really is that simple. If you want to lead your children and your home, turn toward your family. Turn toward your wife and your kids. Prefer them above any opportunity you will receive. Prefer them over the paycheck, the status, the stuff. Prefer them when they don't know how to prefer you. You have to desire to rewrite history and not repeat in your family whatever you haven't redeemed in your own story. If you don't make a change, you condemn your kids to repeat the same broken cycles in their stories.

Malachi 4:6 calls us to turn our hearts toward home. Fathers, go first. Don't demand that your kids do it right if you've refused to teach them how. I don't care if they don't want to listen, if they would rather play video games and watch YouTube. You sit them down (or how about just sitting and watching them play the video game they're so good at), you take them out, you engage with them, and you call them up, because you prefer them to anything else you could be doing, and your time with them is so short.

Then, when we've done this in such a way that it's undeniable in our kids' lives, we can see the second half of the verse in Malachi become a reality: *then* the hearts of the children turn toward their fathers. We've placed burdens on our children that we refuse to bear ourselves, and then we complain about it when they act up. Our job is to lead them, not demand things of them. Your children are not employees. They need direction and boundaries and discipline, of course. But in order for any of that to work, they first need a father present whose heart is turned toward them.

THE WORK

Let's end with a few lines from a poem called "Letter to a Dead Father" by Richard Shelton. Take a moment to grab your notebook, a pen or a highlighter, and then read the lines quoted here. As you read, pay attention to your body. Also pay attention to any word or phrase that moves you, and circle or highlight it.

In the poem, Shelton asks, "Do you see now that fathers who cannot love their sons have sons who cannot love?"[4]

What kind of reaction does that line elicit in you? Write it down. Shelton then goes on to say that this was not his father's fault, or his own. How does that idea strike you?

He ends his poem by saying, "I needed your love but I recovered without it. Now I no longer need anything."[5]

What kind of response do you have to these ending lines? Also write down why you think any specific phrase or word moved you. There are no right or wrong answers; just write in this book or continue noting in your journal what you think or feel. Don't judge yourself. Silence the inner critic and allow yourself simply to write down whatever it is that comes to mind.

Lastly, no matter your age or marital status, consider at least one way to turn your heart toward home. Write it down, and then do it before you move onto the next chapter.

Path 4

Listening to the Call of Adventure

> It's a dangerous business, Frodo, going out your door. You step onto the road, and if you don't keep your feet, there's no knowing where you might be swept off to.
>
> —J. R. R. Tolkien, *The Fellowship of the Ring*

Every boy hears it when he is young. It's as if boys come out of the womb with it beating in their chest and pumping through their veins—the call into the wild. Into an adventure they know in their souls they were made to experience. The places, the people, the experiences, the narrow escapes from evil forces, and the crucial friendships they will make along the way.

Yet adventure is robbed from boys and men rather quickly in life today, especially when we are left without mentors and parents who urge us to explore. Most of our life these days seems hidden behind the safety of our phones, our iPads, our computers, our TVs, our safe little screens in sterilized spiritual experiences with no confrontation or courage involved. No mystery, no questions; just pathetic, weak answers that can never stand up to the grit of real life, and every man knows it. Men might avoid saying it and become disappointed or embittered. They might misidentify it or run from it, but they know. They know there has to be more than what they are being sold by governments, church leaders, well-meaning pastors, protective mothers, and scared fathers. Most men never leave the safety of their mother's breast and have never been given the opportunity to travel beyond their father's limitations or lack of presence.

That's why Jesus gave us such a simple call: "Come." That's it.

He said "I am the way" and "Come," and then at the end of His life, before His ascension, He said "Go." This is the call to adventure, in simple language, right from Scripture. Jesus Christ says, "I am the way. Come, follow Me. Now go and do the same things I did, whether you feel Me near you or not."

That may be some paraphrasing on my part, but you can see the emphasis. Life is supposed to be about adventure, about following God into the unknown and trusting Him. Then we turned all that into safe, textbook religious experiences. From healing and evangelism to preaching and prophecy, we attempt to build guardrails around people through our own fears, and we then call it theology or ministry. It's no longer adventure; it's duty. It's another veiled attempt to please a father who is absent, in the hope that I will perform well enough to get his attention, and in turn he will give me the affection I so desperately desire.

There has to be more than this. Those paths only lead to greater ego and more entitlement for men who can parrot the "right" language and perform appropriately, while the rest of us get left behind because we won't comply with such low and obviously broken attempts to reach heaven. Does that make us rebellious? I hope not. There are thousands of men who love God and want to serve Him sitting along the back row of churches, but the opportunities they're being offered and the communities they're being invited into lack the visceral engagement required to pull them into something bigger than themselves.

For most men I've worked with, it's not their lack of willingness to go. They want to go, desperately, but they feel as if no one has pointed in a direction and said "Go." It feels as if everyone else is just trying to convince men to stay put and be on their "team" and serve their "dream"—in the name of Jesus, of course. So many men have simply submitted to this because nothing better is being offered to them, so their journey stops far short of what it was meant to be. Most of us have had our ability to look up stolen from us. We've forgotten what it is to look to the sky and see possibility. We know religion, we know Scripture, and we know the difference between right and wrong, good and evil. But is that it?

▼ ▼ ▼

Parzival grew in that forest, whittling arrows and bows, as if his father were still alive and whispering to him from a distant place he couldn't see or attend. Even with the dense forest all around him, consumed in the deep hues of greens and browns, the occasional burst of blue would break along the treetops to reveal an endless sky. His gaze would be drawn upward, into a world deep inside himself that he didn't have language to express. A world filled with the chatter of birds that called him beyond his borders. Their simple, devoted songs filled him, and he wished he could leave the ground and soar upward to see what they could see. (As Martin Shaw would say, "the boy got dreamt."[1])

Parzival took this longing to his mother and told her of the bird songs and his desires. But she brushed them off and pulled him down to earth with duty and daily chores. He brought his dreams to his mother enough times, however, that her fears were ignited. She ordered the woodsmen of a nearby village to strangle all the birds so that the forest fell silent, and the boy's young heart grew dim once again.

Parzival's mother pushed him into even more religious training than before. She laid out before him the foundations of sin and atonement, God and the devil, angels and demons. The world for him became black and white, dualistic in its core, and he wanted to be "good" for the sake of his mother and the great sorrow she bore. He listened to her every word as gospel truth and questioned none of it.

▾ ▾ ▾

In order to cross into the adventure you were made for as a man, there must be a confrontation with the feminine, in the form of your mother. The feminine ideals and values of a mother will not carry you into the masculine realm for which you were created. This doesn't make your mother wrong or bad. Remember that engaging with our story doesn't mean we have to make heroes and villains. We all have both potentials inside us; the goal is to lean toward the good.

Two Mothering Archetypes

In mythology there are two archetypes for *mother*. These are the "Great Mother" and the "Devouring Mother," two sides of the same coin. In fact, you can see one side in Scripture very clearly. Wisdom is always referred to as a woman because "she" is carrying that which you need in order to help you become who you were meant to become and live the life you were always meant to live. This is the "Great Mother" and the feminine side of our Creator made manifest in our midst. It's important to understand these two archetypes of mother as we journey into the world as men, to unravel the twisted knot of advice given to us by those who meant well but regardless did damage to us. It does not have to be labeled as "bad" or "good," but it does need

70

to be true. For a man this journey begins when he leaves the care and covering of his mother and is able to address that which was helpful and that which was hurtful in his connection to her, and she must allow him to do so as he embraces his masculinity.

A mother operating from this archetype of the Great Mother is able to nurture without controlling. She is able to offer emotional support without making it about her, and she creates flexible boundaries that allow her young boy to scrape his knees exploring the world while she still makes sure he doesn't run into oncoming traffic. She provides open encouragement and affirmation about who her child is and who he is becoming. This mother is able to allow a boy to become who he is, despite how she may be working through her own trauma and engaging with her own wounds. This requires a great deal of work and maturity on the mother's part, but it is absolutely possible and offers the greatest opportunities to her children, especially for a young son in becoming the man he was created to be.

But many men encounter the Devouring Mother in their childhood instead. Her boundaries are rigid and cannot be questioned. She offers no encouragement, only criticism and condemnation. This leaves a young boy determined to perform better to receive the nurturing he so desperately requires from the feminine touch and feminine voice. A mother of this archetype uses the language of "protection," but the young boy doesn't even know what he's being protected from, because he hasn't shared his mother's pain and loss. If her pain and loss came when the boy was old enough to watch and see, however, and perhaps even experience it with her, the boy will become his mother's defender, assuming the role of protector and caretaker because the father left, passed away, or was abusive. That was never supposed to be a young man's role.

Everything in the realm of the Devouring Mother is micromanaged under her scrutiny and control. Her authority is ultimate, and her punishments are swift, usually involving a rejection of the young boy in some way, withholding love so he is forced to earn it back. This cycle can continue throughout a son's entire life, even when he is grown up and has family of his own.

The Devouring Mother will use guilt and shame to coerce her son back into her arms and under her control. In most cases the mother doesn't want to be that way, and she doesn't even see it in herself (unless she's a narcissist; then she does it on purpose). This cycle stems from her own unresolved pain and hurt from her past, which she has refused to deal with. It wasn't an evil force that removed the sweet songbirds from the forest of Parzival's youth; it was his own mom. She didn't do it because she hated Parzival; she did it from a distorted view of love that was forged in the fire of her own pain.

As we move into the adventure of our lives, we will wrestle with the tension of a mother or feminine figure who moved between these two images. The Devouring Mother side of her that was birthed from her own pain and trauma and the Great Mother side that cared and comforted us as we were released into the world. It is hard for mothers to watch their young boys grow into men. It is a painful process to be separate from the feminine and to learn to embrace the masculine for both the mother and the child, but if the mother does not allow her son to move into manhood then he will begin to rebel or make himself ugly to her so that she rejects him and he gets the separation his undeveloped masculinity needs to find the adventure he was made for.

The Effects of a "Mother Wound"

Maybe you grew up under the influence of a Devouring Mother. Or maybe you didn't have a mother. Or maybe it wasn't your father who left, but your mother. This kind of environment over the course of your young development will have created a "mother wound." Like the father wound we talked about earlier, this is the space created in our lives and stories that allows for lies and distortions to enter because it was never properly covered by our mother. For men, this can lead to devastating behaviors and views of women.

Several things occur when a man has an unresolved or unaddressed mother wound. He can become completely reliant on women and reject the masculine realm altogether because the safety and "protection" of his devouring mom is all he has ever known, and now it's all he ever wants. Such men live in a state of romantic idealism, looking for the perfect mate and a relationship involving high emotion and high drama. When these cease or normalize he moves on, whether he is married or not, to look for the next big emotional romp through the weeds with someone who "gets him."

A man with a mother wound can also become highly emotionally dependent on women to meet all his needs. When they fail to deliver, he becomes angry and resentful toward women in general for not being available to take care of him. These men need to be constantly encouraged and mothered by their wives and girlfriends, which might be cute for a few months while dating, but turns into a nightmare for both individuals a handful of years into a marriage.

Then finally, in the realm of sexuality, men with a mother wound may experience a degree of shame around their body and their desires for sex. Early on, they were so criticized for what they wanted or longed for that later even sex falls into a category of wanting something for themselves, which cycles them into shame and guilt whenever the topic arises or they have to discuss it in their marriage.

This is not a comprehensive list of the effects of father wounds and mother wounds, and these things manifest in varying degrees based on the severity of the individual experience and personality of the man experiencing them. I am simply attempting to expose you to some of the signs of wounding you may be able to see in your own life, so you can begin to give them care and attention and so they do not define your adventure and keep you from it. This is the beauty of owning your story and doing the work; you are not a slave to your emotions or behaviors. No more thinking *I'm never going to get over this* or *I can never change*. Once you know the root system underneath where your pain came from, you can change how you react to it when it shows up in your marriage, with your kids, at your job, and yes, even in church.

Can a mother or father wound be covered by a surrogate, perhaps an aunt, uncle, grandmother, grandfather, stepparents, or adoptive parents? Absolutely. But there will be scars; there will be wounds from the lack of a biological connection. And there will be pain that must be addressed, or it will attempt to define your future relationships and your ability to engage with your story in a way that is helpful. Even young men in loving and nurturing stepfamilies or adoptive families carry a higher risk of dealing with depression or anxiety.[2] This is why it's so important for husbands and wives to do the work in their marriage. The effect trickles down to their children.

Launched from Liminal Spaces

When a husband and wife are connected in the home, serving their family together with their unique skills and perspectives, they are able to offer a well-rounded experience for a boy attempting to find his way in the world. There will come a moment when a young boy has an experience that calls him into who he was meant to be, and as parents we must build the place from which he can launch.

▼ ▼ ▼

Parzival had walked from his mother's hut into the forest, as was his daily custom, to gather berries, small game for the table, and bits of kindling for the fire. On his walks he was always gazing up at the trees, searching for a hint of blue breaking between the deep green of the branches.

But on this day, as his feet trod the same ground they had trod a thousand times before, something new could be heard in the distance. Low at first, it sounded like thunder approaching, perhaps a storm coming in from some distant stretch of sky. The low rumbles carried with them the sound of clanking metal against metal. As the sound grew louder, Parzival felt a startling rumble beneath his feet, as if the ground itself were coming to swallow him whole.

His mother had taught him of angels and demons. She had warned him of devils that had come from some dark place beyond our understanding and wandered on the earth. She had told him of their dark powers and their hunger for death, and he knew this was what was coming for him.

The sound grew and became almost deafening, undiscernible in direction, closing in on him with each moment. Louder and louder, as if it were coming from within himself. Parzival instinctually dove behind a tree, shivering with fright, the full weight of his body pressed against the rough flesh of the oak that would hopefully be his salvation. He closed his eyes and prayed to God what he thought would be his last prayer.

Then through the tree line burst three knights on horseback, like the sun at dawn, beaming with grace and glory from another age. An age where men defied evil for the sake of nobility, overthrew kingdoms for the sake of chivalry, and stood against unjust governments for the sake of the crown and flag. An age where women were honored and revered. An age where magic was still in the air and heaven was still on the tongue of every living thing.

Parzival had never seen anything like this. He knew of the grimy hunters who wandered the forest, but these were not men like them. He knew that if they weren't demons, they had to be angels, just as his mother had said. So he ran from his cover, bowed before them, and began to cry out in worship.

The leader of this band of knights smiled, and they all chuckled kindly before he corrected the young boy. "Young sir, we are not of heaven. We are of Camelot. Just men, Knights of Arthur's Round Table, in pursuit of a nefarious villain who has taken a fair maiden from our land."

Parzival had never heard of such a place and knew nothing of such men. Everything the knight was telling him was of foreign origin. He stuttered and stumbled though his questions, and the knight patiently explained everything to him—the kingdom of Camelot, the crown, the knights, the quests, the courts.

Parzival could only stare, struck by the power and majesty of the scene laid out before him. The fog over his eyes, from his time spent in the forest under the grief of his mother, was now lifting. He was waking up.

The knight could see it and sensed something of raw quality in the young man, so he spoke up: "Go to Camelot and train as a knight. The world is full of adventure waiting for you to answer the call. This journey won't be easy, but hear this: if that which you seek does not require sacrifice, then it is not worth pursuing."

Parzival was too young, too immature in the ways of the world to comprehend what the knight had just given him. All he heard was the invitation; all he wanted was to be like these men. He knew that he *must* find his way to Camelot.

With that, the knights bid Parzival farewell, and they roared from that place with the same ferocity with which they had arrived.

Silence.

▼ ▼ ▼

In myth. the wilderness is not a place where you are lost. It's a place of transition, of opportunity. It's a liminal space where we cross over and the possibilities become endless. I love the following definition of liminal space, adapted from Father Richard Rohr's writing on the subject:

Liminal space is an inner state and sometimes an outer situation where we can begin to think and act in new ways. It is where we are betwixt and between, having left one room or stage of life but not yet entered the next. We usually enter liminal space when our former way of being is challenged or changed— perhaps when we lose a job or a loved one, during illness, at the birth of a child, or a major relocation. It is a graced time, but often does not feel "graced" in any way. In such space, we are not certain or in control. . . .

The very vulnerability and openness of liminal space allows room for something genuinely new to happen.[3]

I believe we enter spaces like this many times over the course of our lives, but we are never taught to be attuned to them, so we miss them or walk right past them. They are burning bush opportunities that we don't turn aside for—not because we're rebellious or attempting to reject them, but because no one ever taught us or told us that these spaces were available to us.

Then, when we unknowingly step into one of these liminal spaces, all of a sudden anything can happen, and anything is possible. We are immediately called to let go of who we were and start believing for who we could be.

"Drop your nets," Jesus told the men He was calling, "and come follow Me" (see Mark 1:16–18). Such a call demands a response, and you won't know the details until you're on your way. That's the nature of true adventure.

Another example of this from pop culture is in the movie *Star Wars*, when young Luke Skywalker finds out who he really is. This wasn't new information; it was confirming what he already knew to be true. From a young age something inside him was always looking up, and he tells his uncle that he wants to be a pilot. He stares at the sky and longs for something buried deep within himself. Then, when he finally flies off with Obi-Wan Kenobi, nobody watching the movie is thinking, *Oh NO, don't do it!* We get excited for him, for the unlimited potential he just tapped into, because we are excited for ourselves, wanting to experience the same thing.

The younger you are, the more you believe anything is possible. As we get older we lose our divine imagination, and in the process we lose hope. But that's the power of the wilderness, of a good adventure—we begin to believe again that anything is possible. Joy begins to invade broken circumstances as we see them as opportunities, not obstacles to overcome.

For the Sake of Adventure

What if that's all a calling is? Not something new being given to you, but a confirmation of what you already knew deep within to be true about yourself What you knew before the trauma, before the rejection, before the hurt and the letdowns, disappointments, and betrayals. It's the child inside you who still knows who you are and what you're capable of, speaking to you in a way that you can still turn and listen to.

What if the burning bush moments of our lives are simply God reminding us of what has always been true about our story, our family, our lives? Isn't that what God speaks through the prophet Jeremiah? "Before I formed you in the womb I knew you" (Jeremiah 1:5). This isn't about acting right, performing well, learning religious language; this is about hearing the voice inside you that never left you even at your worst moments. And you stop running from it and start listening to it, not for the sake of better behavior, but for the sake of adventure. When you are living in the adventure you were made for, you don't have time for distractions. You are fully alive, and so laser focused on the path in front of you that you can't imagine wasting time or energy on anything else.

Neither could Parzival.

▼ ▼ ▼

Parzival stood in awe of the experience that had just found him. The same experience his mother had tried to protect him from since the day of his birth and the loss of her husband. He shook his head, turned his body, and began a full sprint back to his home, back to his mother. He caught her hanging the laundry in the back of their small hut, and he told her every detail of the encounter with the knights and his invitation to Camelot.

As he finished recounting the event, his mother passed out in the same dramatic fashion you might imagine from a stage actress. She fell, and not just from the news that her son was now bringing her. She fell under the weight of her failure. She lay on that damp, mossy forest floor covered in pain only a mother knows. She would not be able to stop him from his journey, and she could not cover the noble blood that now stirred in his veins.

As Herzeloyde rose from the ground and gathered her strength, she did the only thing a loving mother in her position could do: she gave her son a twisted knot of advice that would humiliate him in the eyes of the court and send him back into her arms as soon as possible.

She didn't see her actions that way, of course. To her, this was simply protection, not manipulation. So she spoke with boldness and certainty: "Son, if you must go, then you must hear me out. I know where it is you are about to head, and there are rules you must follow, things you must know as you stretch out into the world. You will need a donkey to ride and a homespun tunic to wear made from sackcloth from our home. Some may say this is the robe of a fool, but I would tell you that you

79

never want to appear too flashy and grandiose before a king of Arthur's stature and nobility. Show some humility in his presence, and keep a quiet dignity about you. Remember to go to church every day. There you will find provision for your journey and rest for your body. Always take advice from gray-haired men, and if you meet a woman, show respect. This is the chivalric code. Wrestle the ring from the lady's finger, claim it as yours, do not be shy, and kiss and embrace her immediately. Cross the river at the lowest point. All other spots are treacherous in nature. And know this: you are of noble birth."

That final piece was the deepest truth she knew about her son, even if her pain would not allow her to teach him how to steward it. Without a father in his life, Parzival had no one to send him out with confidence, with a clear sense of who he was and what he could accomplish. His mother wanted him home and young forever, safe under her nurturing care and watchful eye. She desired to keep him close and protected under her roof. No adventures, no quests, no maidens, no grails, no knights, no danger. So she gave him her advice, some helpful, some not, to give him the life she thought would be best for him. With the wisdom she provided, he would remain safe as he went—and he would be laughed out of the courts the moment they saw him. Then he would return to her with the quest and knighthood out of his system, and they could continue their life in the forest, hidden from any further disruptions and dangerous invitations.

Parzival's final night at home was restless for both mother and son. She sewed his ragged cloak as he tossed and turned with nervous excitement, awaiting what the next day might bring.

He arose with the sun, threw on the tunic his mother had sewn for him through the night, took the small pack of supplies she had prepared, and grabbed the small javelin he had used since he was a boy to track small game through thorn and thicket. He kissed his mother's tear-soaked cheek as he mounted the disastrous-looking little donkey with pride, kicked it in the sides, and began to trot away, never looking back.

If Parzival had turned even for a moment to look behind him, what he'd have seen would have stopped him from ever leaving that place. For as he left, his mother fell to the forest floor, dead from a broken heart.

▼ ▼ ▼

When you step into the adventure of your life, a lot of well-meaning people will be looking to give you advice. I can promise you that no matter who the person is or what role he or she has in your life, not all of it will be good advice. I don't care if it's your parents, your pastor, a leader, a preacher, the barber, or your grandfather. They can only see the world from their perspective, which for all of us is severely limited based on our own personal experience. Our goal is to humbly receive from those we have invited to speak into our lives, and then use discernment to see what will help and what will hinder. (If unsolicited advice is given from the uninvited, you can usually throw that away immediately.)

In Parzival's youthful zeal, he wandered off without questioning anything his mother had told him; he was just excited to go. This has happened to many of us, and when the disappointment hits from following the faulty advice of others, many of us default into depression or rejection, never attempting to step out again. Or we stop trusting any authority, to avoid potential pain. But all we need is a filter to put the advice through in order to develop better discernment. I would offer you three sources for this filtering process: the Word, a witness, and wisdom.

When growing in discernment as men, we have to become acquainted with the Word. I'm not saying we need to be Bible scholars or theologians, but we do need to understand the fundamental characteristics of God, as revealed in Scripture, in order to know when someone is offering us something contrary to His nature and Spirit. If the advice we are being handed

81

doesn't line up with what we know and what we've read in His Word, then we can let it go.

We also need a witness, someone who knows us and has a history with us. Allow the person who is your witness to hear the advice you've been given, and seek his or her opinion on it. Does it feel to your witness like something consistent with who he or she knows you to be, or with the season you are in?

Finally, pass all advice through the filter of wisdom, your personal experience, and who you know yourself to be. You know what you've been through, and you know what you believe. Does this advice contradict that experience? If so, you can let it go.

Without these filters, Parzival is setting himself up for trouble in our story. But so are we, when we blindly accept the words of others at face value and then try to make those words fit into our circumstance.

There is also one last sad detail in this portion of our story that all men must face: You must leave the realm of the feminine in order to fully enter the world of the masculine, and this will "kill" your mother.

I obviously don't mean that literally; this is coming from a mythological story, after all. What we know is that in order to become a man, a young boy has to come under the influence of a father or a group of men in order to walk fully into manhood. The influence of a mother does remain; it is treasured and there will be an eventual reuniting of these two energies. But you cannot learn masculine principles and practices in a predominately feminine environment.

I wonder if that's why so many men have a difficult time connecting in church. The romantic language of our songs, our practices, and our prayers don't lead most men into the conviction and courage they long for. Therefore they serve, they give, they listen, and then they go home. I think many men love God, love their wives, love their kids, and love their communities, but how they express that love doesn't fit into most churches, where the framework for love and devotion is primarily based in romanticism, a type of love driven by feelings. That's not an excuse not to engage, however. I'm not giving you an out. I just want to challenge you as we move ahead to explore new ways to dive deeper into your own experience with God.

THE WORK

I want you to grab your journal and answer this question: *What are your spiritual practices?*

Let me define what I'm looking for. I'm going to give you five areas that are commonly known as "spiritual practices," which will help every man as he begins to live out the call to adventure on his life. Write in your journal how you personally would like to "practice" each one. I'm emphasizing practice because that's what it is, *practice*. This is not a competition. This is not pass or fail. This is progress over perfection. It's taking simple growth steps each day. So not only are we going to define your spiritual practices; you are also going to determine how and when you're going to step out and practice.

Start small, a few minutes a day of meditation, a fast of something simple that you know will be a struggle, but that you can manage for one day. If you set the bar too high too quickly, you will feel disappointment and will want to try over again. So refrain from trying to be the best at a specific task, and simply try to be the best you.

Here are the practices I'd like you to explore:

1. *Prayer*
    Prayer is asking, not just conversation. Throughout Scripture, people prayed for that which they desired

from God. We are starting here not because God is a vending machine, but because He is kind. I know there are lots of other forms of prayer besides making requests, but it is being vulnerable to tell God specifically what you're asking for and what you need.

2. *Meditation*

This word scares a lot of men, but it's biblical, and it's simple to do in small chunks as we begin. Sit in a chair or on the floor, hands in your lap, eyes closed. Take ten slow breaths in through the nose, and then out through the mouth. As you breathe out, repeat a simple prayer in your mind. I like the prayer offered in Psalm 23: "The LORD is my Shepherd; I have all that I need" (verse 1, NLT). If you don't like that one, just open the book of Psalms and choose a line you like. Make sure you repeat the same line for all ten slow breaths. Then, on the last breath, hold your breath as long as you can (usually about sixty seconds is good), and relax your whole body. *Slow down.*

3. *Fasting*

Just start small. Choose one thing to give up one day a week. If you start with that, I promise you the impact on your soul will be huge. We don't fast to change God; we fast to change ourselves. Fasting reminds us of what longing feels like. If we do it regularly, we develop a longing for more than just what we give up; we begin to feel a longing for God that we may never have experienced before.

4. *Reading*

Just spend a few minutes each day with the Word. I don't care what translation or what book of the Bible; just read a few passages a day, and as the spiritual

covering of your house, you will see transformation
in your heart and home. Reading is a simple practice
that allows your mind, your heart, and your home to
be washed by the Word on a regular basis. If you don't
know where to begin, I recommend the books of Psalms
or Proverbs in the Old Testament, or the books of John
or Acts in the New Testament.

5. *Journaling*

At this point in our journey, you should already be
journaling, which we covered in the first chapter. (If you
need a review, just head back to The Work section at
the end of chapter 1.)

Path 5

Stumbling Forward in Immaturity

The mark of the immature man is that he wants to die nobly for a cause, while the mark of the mature man is that he wants to live humbly for one.

—Wilhelm Stekel

We have two things working against us when we begin our journey from boyhood to manhood. The first is that we are all full of male energy and potential, without the ability to view our own immaturity. The second is the bad advice we have been given by well-meaning individuals along the way. The first blinds us to our own inability and lack of experience. The second gives us the impression that we know things we don't, all because someone we trusted convinced us that he or she knew something of the world, when actually they learned it through disappointment, not development.

So there we are, young and naive, convinced of our own rightness and running headlong into an adventure we couldn't possibly comprehend, not even paying attention to the bodies we leave in our wake. And although it seems we should do something about that, the truth is that in ourselves and in others, this is a major part of the growth process. We must learn what we don't know by walking into circumstances and relationships that will expose our lack without killing us.

Think back through your own life. Did you learn the most by sitting in pews and classrooms, or by fumbling through life's situations and testing the things you've heard to see which produces fruit and which produces frustration? Every book you've read, podcast you've listened to, or YouTube video you've watched was all from the perspective of one individual. Regardless of that person's platform or position, it will remain his or her opinion. Each perspective can be helpful or hurtful, depending on the context and circumstance it is applied to. But we cannot simply take everything we receive as truth, even if it moves us deeply. Doing that is a clear sign of immaturity and will hinder us as we attempt to move forward and grow.

Many of us already find ourselves worn out and disappointed at the lack of transformation we have experienced from all the information we've taken in, and frustrated by all the wasted time and money we've invested. But that's the cost of blindly attempting to apply the advice we've been given, without proper filtering or critique. Again, as we talked about in the previous chapter, it's vital that we filter other people's advice through the Word, a witness, and wisdom. If we don't use those filters, we miss divine opportunities laid out before us and create chaos everywhere behind us, due to our lack of maturity.

▼ ▼ ▼

As Parzival left his mother's home and proceeded into the forest farther than he had ever gone before, it was as if the forest went with him and the animals stayed in stride with each hoofprint of the donkey. With the sun caressing the back of his neck, he happened upon a large tent the likes of which he had never seen before—such size, such beauty, such a flag, and such pageantry surrounding it. He assumed it was a beautiful church laid out before him, a house of worship and provision for his journey, exactly as his mother said he would come upon. He had never seen a church for himself, but he thought that with the grandiose nature of what he was now seeing, how could it be anything less?

The young boy expectantly entered through the great marquee and found a great feast spread out on a grand table on one side of the sprawling venue. On the other side in a bed across the way was a beautiful woman, Jeschute, her skin as white as the swan on the pool at night. Her hair flowed across her chest between her bosom like a great, dark stream freeing itself from two mountain passes. Her honeyed curves aroused him in a fashion he had not previously known. This wasn't lust; it was the purest form of arousal and appreciation for beauty he had ever known in his young male life. As she slept, he approached her the way his mother had said. Noticing the ring on her finger, he came over to her, wrestled it away, and kissed her awkwardly and forcefully.

Jeschute awoke, and quite a skirmish ensued. Parzival claimed the ring and then headed to the table to have his fill. As he did, she attempted to explain that the ring was from Orilus, a knight who was courting her, and that this feast was intended as a celebration for her beloved knight's return this very day. She pleaded for Parzival to give her ring back and leave, but all he saw was everything his mother had said: provision, the maiden, the church. All was laid out before him, so he must be on the right path.

The maiden saw that he was a very different sort of man than she had encountered before. He didn't try to take advantage of her; he was simple, almost holy. So with a little more convincing, she escorted him from the tent just before her knight returned. When Orilus came to the tent, found her without a ring, and saw that the banquet had been eaten, he determined that she had been unfaithful. He vowed to kill whoever the knight was who had stolen the ring from his maiden. Parzival knew nothing of this and continued on his way.

▼ ▼ ▼

When the mistakes we make along the way are not from rebellion but from our lack of experience, we find ourselves able to align with what mythologists call the "holy fool." Parzival is often referred to in this way because he doesn't know what he doesn't know and he steps forward anyway, learning from his mistakes and never taking himself too seriously. I don't mean that he thinks he's a joke; he simply moves forward with a childlike confidence, unpretentious in his nature, which allows him to be led by his heart rather than by social expectations. He may be unsure of where the next step will take him, but he's convinced that there is endless opportunity laid out before him in all directions. This boyhood vision of life will be tempered into something more useful in the future, but for now he can see himself as unlimited potential. Maybe that's why Jesus calls us to be like children and be born again. When we lose that ability in our lives through tragedy or trauma, we lose a part of ourselves that we require to walk fully into our masculinity.

No Idea What to Do

I love my wife. I have from the first day I met her. But for the first eight years of our marriage, I had no idea what to do with this beautiful creature God had gifted me. I wanted to steward her heart, her dreams, her love in a way that honored who she was and who she would become over our lifetime together. But I failed miserably. Not because I wasn't a good man or wasn't making attempts; it was simply because I didn't know what I was doing.

I wasn't trying to hurt Nicci or make her feel abandoned, but I did, all while I pursued what I believed was my calling. I left her completely behind. The worst part is that I didn't even know it was happening. I know how that makes me sound, but I know so many men in the same position as I was, blindly damaging our most precious relationships because we simply don't know what to do or where to start.

So let me give it to you: it all begins when you can admit, first to yourself and then to others, that you have no idea what you're doing. For men, this is the worst prescription they could ever receive because it means you must embrace vulnerability and let others see you in your weakness, not your strength. But let me offer you some kindness. In the days we live in, it's highly likely that no one ever taught you how to do connection, intimacy, and relationships well. So you've been stumbling along, hoping it would all just "work out" one day and you'd wake up to a thriving, intimate relationship with your wife, a close, caring relationship with your kids, and deep, meaningful relationships with your friends.

Yet it will never happen that way. Every one of these relationships and connections requires different tools and different training. If no one ever showed you what to do, then you can stop beating yourself up for all the damage you've done. This isn't an excuse to just brush over it and not do the work of repair, but it minimizes the voices of shame and guilt and allows you to have a starting point you can grow from.

▾ ▾ ▾

As Parzival wandered dreamily along his path, he came upon another woman crouched behind a large rock, crying uncontrollably. As he approached her, he offered a cheery "God be with you." This caused the woman to look up from her sorrow and take notice of the boy. She wiped her tears and told how she had just found out that her husband died in a joust while fighting a war in a foreign land. As she looked upon the rugged beauty of the boy, she asked him, "What is your name?"

He answered, "My mother simply called me Beautiful Son."

91

At this, her countenance changed and she exclaimed, "You must be Parzival!" And although we have used his name several times in the telling, this would be the first time our young protagonist would hear it for himself.

The woman went on to explain that she was his cousin, Sigune. She spent the next hour describing to him the lineage he had come from. She talked of his noble birth, and of his father—why he had left and how he had died. She told him that her husband had died defending the same lands as Parzival's father.

Again Parzival's immaturity was revealed as he simply thanked her for the information and her kindness, swearing that he would avenge her husband when he found the knight who had killed him. At that, he continued on his way. Camelot was calling, and there was no need to stay with a grieving widow.

▾ ▾ ▾

This is one of the most difficult parts of stumbling forward into manhood when you have no idea what you're doing. Our immaturity causes us to miss the grief that is speaking to us. This young cousin offers Parzival a chance to hear his name and his story, engage with the pain of where he has been, and recognize how it defines where he's going. But he misses it. In the story of Parzival it's Sigune, fully given to her grief, who invites our young hero to engage with his wounds and his sorrow, and to mourn with her. But in his immaturity, all he can see is his potential for greatness. "Camelot is calling," so he moves on.

We miss it too. We can attempt to avoid grief, vainly try to run from it, but that doesn't make it go away. It just delays the very thing we are longing for—to know who we are and what we were made for. Instead of embracing the name we were given, we spend our lives attempting to make a name for ourselves. We use religious language like a "calling" to justify our fears of looking backward or inward at where we came from. But if we are unable to go back where we came from with something of healing and redemption, then did we really go on to have an adventure? Or was it just a frail attempt at avoidance, running from our pain in a culture addicted to comfort and the mantras that "if it feels good, it must be God" and "if it's hard or hurts, it must be the devil," never valuing the grief necessary to find ourselves at the doors of our own destiny?

Who Are You Really, Wanderer?

You were born at the right place, in the right time, in the right family, in the right city, in the right circumstances in all of human history, to bring God the most glory with your life. He doesn't make mistakes, and He doesn't waste anything.

In fact, even others misusing their free will to hurt you, minimize you, push you down, and push you around will be taken into account. Your pain, when yielded to the process, will always reveal the promise you were meant for.

William Stafford spoke about this in his poem called "A Story That Could Be True." He starts the poem by exploring what it would be like if you never knew your real mother or father. What if you didn't know your lineage and didn't know the name you were supposed to have? Would you spend your whole life wondering who you are?

Stafford finishes the poem with these powerful lines: "Who are you really, wanderer? . . . Maybe I'm a king."[1]

Who are you really? Think about it—no matter how abandoned you may have felt, no matter how alone, no matter what life has handed you.

Maybe you are a king.

Maybe that's what this is all about.

Maybe you have more to offer the world, your family, and your kids than you've been told.

Maybe you are actually a son of the living God.

Maybe you have a choice to be something more than you are today.

Maybe you are not a slave to your circumstances.

Maybe you don't have to stay in the same patterns.

Maybe, just maybe, there is more for you.

Letting Grief Lead to Transformation

In order to get to who you might possibly be, why don't we try a new tactic? What if we let grief lead for a little while and see where it takes us? What are the things that move you into sadness? You may not know the answer right off the bat, but think about your mom, your dad, your life circumstances, your wife and kids if you're married. When you've given it adequate invitation and attention, do any of them move you toward sadness, even a little? Or what about your childhood? Is there a season, an event, a situation that floats toward grief or sadness when you think about it? Then simply ask this question: *Why? Why does this make me sad?*

Engage with what you normally avoid and see if it can lead you to places you've never been. When you get there, let yourself feel the sadness that has always been inside. We still have a little way to go in this chapter and in our story, and we'll look more closely at engaging in the work of grief in chapter 10. But if you need to stop here for a moment to allow yourself to process, please do it. As part of the process, once you've found a small space of tenderness, write it down. This is simply a first step toward looking at your experience and seeing the goodness of God and resurrection of Jesus in the midst of your own life. Talk with God about your experience. Ask the Holy Spirit to bring comfort to you as you learn to wrestle with the insights that come from this experience. Jesus understands and relates

94

to your suffering because He has known suffering. Don't rush this. Stay with it longer than you are comfortable; it will build new muscles to combat the avoidance so many men are prone to when doing this work. And last thing, remember to be kind to yourself in this process. These weren't tools you were given as a young boy, so how would you expect to know them?

If you find yourself getting frustrated with the process, just slow down, take a few breaths, and sit in it for a few moments before you move on. Take a break; just don't run from it.

Transformation will only come to the degree to which we are willing to face truth.

If you want surface-level healing, then you don't have far to go. But if you want to walk in the fullness you were created for, the fullness that was robbed from you, then you must go bone deep, to the very marrow of your experience. Let grief have a seat at the table before you move forward. Don't leave it on the side of the road awkwardly as you move on toward whatever it is you want.

▼ ▼ ▼

As the great castle at the center of Camelot came into view in the distance, Parzival's donkey was drooping under his weight, and the stench of the boy's sweat was hanging thickly around him. Parzival noticed in the field ahead a knight adorned in chestnut armor, more vibrant than anything he had ever seen. It was as red as blood and as powerful as a mountain. He could barely look upon the armor, for it shone like the sun.

He approached and asked the knight if this was Camelot and where he could find King Arthur. Clutching a cup from Arthur's own table, the Red Knight exclaimed, "I took this from Arthur and spilled its wine all over Guinevere myself. If you're going to the court, give them my apologies for that. I challenged them to take me on over a land dispute. I have no need for money. I want what is mine and none of them have answered,

95

so their fame lags in a ditch I have dug. Tell them to come out and fight me like men, to defend their king or leave him in disgrace."

Dazzled by the Red Knight and informed by his insults, Parzival journeyed on. When he entered through the gate, no one paid him any attention. Where he was longing to see civility and assurance, he found chaos and disorder. Camelot was in an uproar because of the Red Knight's insults, so Parzival was able simply to wander directly into the center of Arthur's court, right up to his table. The smell of roasting meat and the sound of politics—to Parzival it was as if glory itself filled the air. Great tapestries adorned the walls; beautiful chairs and furniture the likes of which he had never seen filled the halls.

As men jockeyed for position within the court, making declarations and threats, Parzival moved forward and simply knelt at the feet of King Arthur himself. This rustic, homespun youth knelt staring up into the eyes of the great king of Briton himself, the stalwart legend who led the Knights of the Round Table, King Arthur.

Above all the noise, Parzival shouted greetings and began to explain what the Red Knight had told him. As he spoke, the room became quiet. Arthur listened with no smile, no welcoming eye, but he responded with a clear tone and authoritative candor. He informed the young boy that the Red Knight's name was Ithir, and that his claim was illegitimate. He was feared and loved, however, and no one had the appetite to take him on in battle.

Another knight named Kai spoke up and said they should sacrifice Parzival to Ithir in order to wear him down. "Sacrifice the hounds to kill the bear!" he roared.

That was all the invitation Parzival needed. He began to bound from the room in all his childlike arrogance, declaring that he would defend the honor of the court and King Arthur.

As Parzival made his way through the court, he passed before Lady Cunneware, a woman about whom it was prophesied that she would not laugh until she witnessed the greatest knight in the world in her presence. Setting her eyes on Parzival, she burst into uncontainable laughter.

The entire room gasped, for all knew the prophecy and were amazed at what they were witnessing. They backed away, now transfixed by this young boy as he stopped in his tracks. Even in his immaturity, he knew he had just stepped into something sacred. He wasn't sure what would happen next.

But not everyone celebrated the fulfillment of this prophecy. Kai, who earlier had mocked Parzival, had spent months walking in front of Lady Cunneware after each exploit and every conquest, hoping to move her toward joy. Yet nothing had done that until now. In a fit of jealous rage, Kai raised his hand to her and slapped her, a blow that would have laid out any warrior.

If he had not been in the midst of the court, Parzival would have taken his own javelin and dropped Kai where he stood for this disgraceful and brutal act. But in that moment, as he looked upon Lady Cunneware, he vowed to her that he would take retribution on Kai for his unkind and ungallant display toward her, and that any knight whom he defeated he would send back to Camelot to work in service to her.

As Parzival began to leave the chambers of the Round Table, Arthur shouted to him, "If Ithir is defeated, you may claim the Red Knight's armor as your own and join us at the Round Table!"

▼ ▼ ▼

In our youth, as we walk toward initiation and manhood, we will encounter the same three spaces or energies that Parzival did. They are *arousal*, *grief*, and *aggression*, and each has the power to introduce a young boy to parts of himself he may not yet understand.

A youth's arousal and attraction to the feminine will introduce him to his immaturity in ways nothing else can. As Parzival soon found out, this will be both a physical and spiritual experience. Every boy becomes a fool when standing next to a beautiful woman. Even if he's attempting to look cool, it's a cover, and everyone within one hundred yards knows it, especially the lady.

Our grief is ignored in this season, pushed away and minimized. If not just for survival, we do this so we can chase something else that will make us feel better, even if it's only momentary.

Finally, we come across the image of what we want to become and we engage with our aggression, sitting front row at a rock concert, reading a book, or watching sports or a movie about warriors, heroes, adventure, and sacrifice. We witness the work of our father, the stories of our grandfather, our uncle, a pastor, a friend, whomever, and we see what they have or what they represent and decide, *I want it for myself*. At this point we don't even know what "it" is, but the Red Knight in our story is just like the knights in the forest, only ten times bigger, more charismatic, and enigmatic. When we see this in our lives, something inside us says, *I must have that!* It appears from the outside to be an opportunity to change our stars, and we will do anything to lay hold of it.

Then we take all of this and make our way before the king. In the story it's King Arthur; in eternity it's Jesus. In your story, who is it? Whom have you made king? Now, don't get religious on me. Nobody is looking over your shoulder right now. Look at your life, your experiences, your decisions both public and private. Who is the king you kneel before? Whose blessing are you looking for to move forward with your story, even in the midst of mocking voices? We are all submitted to a king in our lives, and I know we want that to be Jesus alone. But so many of us settle for an earthly voice to give us what we need so that we can be who we want to be.

Hearing the Heavenly Father's Voice

Are you still looking for the father you never had? Are you still defending your dad, saying, "He did the best he could"? At some point, we have to stop defending the people in our lives and own our experiences for what they were. We have to stop deciding who was good, who was bad, who was right, who was wrong, and simply allow our stories to be told for what they are. This is what a mature man does. This journey begins when we stop defending our earthly fathers and start listening to the voice of our heavenly Father. What does He say about who you are? Appendix I at the end of this book includes one hundred "I Am" statements from Scripture about who you are, with all the verse references so you can search it out for yourself.

I also love the prophetic nature of God's voice, the living Word spoken through His people for the encouragement and equipping of His children. Look at the image presented in Lady Cunneware, the "laughing prophetess" who with laughter would mark the greatest knight who ever lived. I love this! It's the image of the "holy fool" all the way through to the end. You don't get applause or awards and may never receive recognition or platforms, but will you bring joy?

Joy marks the greatest warriors in God's Kingdom. Yes, conviction, yes, confidence, yes, courage, yes, wisdom, yes, yes, yes. I get it that you're asking, *Where are all the manly qualities?* But they all start with and sustain joy, and if they don't, then they're for ego.

In fact, men with an ego full of false masculine energy lash out at joy and want to knock it down and suppress it, especially if someone else is releasing joy and they don't have it themselves. But this is still immaturity leading the way. As we stumble toward the power and complexity of true biblical masculinity, and as we move away from the ego-driven, avoidant ways of our youth, then we must encounter joy. Yes, there is grief. Yes, there is suffering and sacrifice. Yet "joy comes with the morning" (Psalm 30:5). This is our promise, this is our pursuit, that we would find on our journey the joy of knowing what the voice of our loving Father sounds like and the courage it gives us to keep moving forward.

THE WORK

So much of understanding who we are and stumbling forward even in our immaturity is about understanding where we came from and what has been passed down to us from family who came before us. Parzival is learning a lot about where he came from, and part of his immaturity is wrapped up in the fact that he has no value for lineage and legacy. He receives his name, his father's name, and where he came from, and he just moves on, no big deal. So many men make a similar mistake when trying to move forward in their journey. They make no effort to explore their lineage, and then they wonder why they behave in ways that are contrary to their desire.

One of the first tools we will use on this journey to avoid that mistake is a genogram. A genogram is a visual representation of a family tree that includes detailed information on relationships, medical history, and behaviors.[2]

Take a moment and visit appendix II, where I have a genogram example drawn out for you, along with simple instructions on how to create your own. Work on that now. The goal is not to be too extensive or exhaustive; this is simply an exploration. Don't dismiss it or pass by it too quickly, however. Pay attention to what was handed down to you, and then ask yourself, *Are there any patterns that emerge?* Do you see cycles of divorce, abuse, or addiction? What about financial favor, foundations of faith, or powerful role models?

We will return to this later in the book, but the goal right now is reference and exposure. Most men have never done anything like this exercise, but doing a genogram will give you something to stand on later as you discover more about yourself and go further into your journey toward maturity.

Path 6

Tempering Aggression through Initiation

> You enter the forest at the darkest point, where there is no
> path. Where there is a way or path, it is someone else's path.
> You are not on your own path. If you follow someone else's
> way, you are not going to realize your potential.
>
> —Joseph Campbell, *The Hero's Journey*

Conformity is the devil's work. It is a vain or fearful attempt
to make us all the same, devoid of depth and personality, robbing us of our unique perspective and insight. You were never
meant to fit in and relinquish the power of your story to make
others feel okay with their own compromise. We can't afford
to numb ourselves to culture just so we can fit in.

This has been one of the most significant problems in the
Church since Constantine's decree at the Edict of Milan in 313. I
believe since that moment the Church has suffered a cataclysmic
shift in its identity. It so readily assumes the values, forms, and

functions of the culture it finds itself in. In the apostolic age, the Church was completely countercultural and anti-imperial in every way. Today, however, we find many within its leadership, and even those all the way down to the pews, who long for social media's validation. Church leaders long for the status of celebrity preachers (not to mention for health and wealth), to prove to themselves that they're having an impact or some measure of success in their Christian walk. This is not cynicism on my part; this has been my experience and the experience of many who have encountered the brokenness found in high levels of Christian leadership within the Church. These realities have filtered down to affect the expectations of what it means to be a man and what it looks like to follow Christ in this postmodern age.

There is another way. Scripture calls us up and out in Romans 12:2 (NIV): "Do not conform to the pattern of this world, but be transformed by the renewing of your mind." The renewing of your mind is not about having a positive outlook or positive mental attitude toward yourself and others. It's so much more. This verse is inviting us to radically change the way we view everything. The word *renew* here is only used in this form two times in the entire New Testament. It is a unique way of stating a complete and total change for the better. This invitation to renew our mind is about altering how we experience our thoughts, our emotions, our purposes, our desires, and even our capacity for spiritual truth and for recognizing good in the world around us.

Transformed is also a unique word in this verse. It is the same word used to describe the transfiguration of Christ in the three Gospel accounts where it appears, which to me is a beautiful sign that when we engage in the process of personal transformation, we begin to look like what we were always supposed to look like. At the transfiguration, Christ is revealed for who He really is, in all His glory. As we do the work of transformation in our own lives by the renewing of our minds, we actually begin to look how we were always meant to—and in turn we look like the One we love. We take on the very likeness of Christ.

You don't resemble Christ simply by doing the things He did. Anyone can go pray for a stranger, go on a mission trip, attend a ministry school, tithe 10 percent, and serve on Sundays. But did you change the way you think and view yourself and the world around you, or is it all a religious show? You will know there's a difference in you when the people around you are able to point it out, the same way the apostles did with Jesus on the mountain. They could physically see Him differently. Has your wife noticed yet? Your friends? Your family? If not, then you may have some good information, but you haven't changed your mind yet. Using new language doesn't mean you have a new mind; transformation means using new ways of engaging with the people around you and the world you live in.

Transformation Begins with Initiation

The beginning of the transformation process is called *initiation*, a symbolic or literal experience that marks the transition from one way of life to another. It's the catalytic event that shakes us free from our slumber and welcomes us back to the land of the living, usually with great force.

In almost every culture on earth and throughout time, you will find that men are not born; they are made. At some pivotal moment, they walked from boyhood into manhood with great care and intention. There was a ritual process, with wise elders who prepared them to embrace the struggles and sacrifices necessary to walk in the fullness of their masculinity—to support a home, raise children, serve a wife, and lead spiritually, but also to manage their emotions and expectations while developing problem-solving skills and clarifying how they would contribute to the common good of their culture.

This was more than a one-time event, although it usually included a rite of passage, some kind of marker to look back at and know you had transitioned into a new way of living. No matter how painful the experience, those scars became a reminder of what you overcame and what you were then capable of. As we talked about in chapter 2, every form of traditional initiation required a "sacred wound," walking to the doors of death and back again, marked by the process in such a significant way that it would be impossible ever to be the same again.

In the heart of the Amazon rainforest, the Sateré-Mawé tribe holds a unique initiation ritual that follows this process of walking boys into manhood through an intentional process passed down from generation to generation. Boys as young as twelve undergo meticulous preparation for the impending rite of passage that will require them to endure pain in ways they have watched so many others endure before them. The process begins as the elders of the tribe venture into the dense jungle, only to return with an unusual bounty from their hunt—bullet ants, known to have one of the most painful stings in the insect world. The women of the tribe prepare the boys as the collected ants are woven into gloves made of leaves, a symbol to every Sateré-Mawé boy of what they must pass through if they want to enter into the adult world.

When the moment arrives, the boys do not shy away. Draped in traditional garb they stand on the precipice of a life-altering experience that will provide the necessary marking to them and the tribe that they can bear the weight of what it means to be a protector and a provider. With each ant-filled glove placed on their hands they must endure the excruciating experience for ten full minutes. As the venom flows through their body, they lose a sense of time and reality as they physically, spiritually, and mentally hang between the tangible and the spiritual. But they are not alone. The rhythmic pounding of drums and the haunting melodies of tribal songs surround them as the candidates engage in traditional dances. They are surrounded by those they love, witnessed as a symbol of strength and resilience as they actively engage with their pain, a visceral reminder that this ordeal is a passage, a symbolic death leading to rebirth. They remove the gloves, and the pain intensifies as they continue dancing and moving with the elders of the tribe by their side, sweating out the toxins over the next twenty-four hours. But this is not the end for those in the Sateré-Mawé tribe who want to cross from boyhood to manhood. This entire process must be done a total of twenty times over the course of their young lives.[1]

We have created a culture that runs from pain, denies its power, and refuses to acknowledge the scars we bear from our experiences. The scars we carry because of the choices we've made and the scars we bear because of those who wronged us and harmed us. But initiation is an invitation into engaging with those scars and that pain in a way nothing else can. Jesus modeled this for us. When He rose from the grave in His resurrected body, He kept His scars. Then with those scars still fresh, three days old, Jesus walks up to "doubting Thomas" and tells him that in order to remove his doubt, he must look upon those wounds and place his life inside them. Jesus doesn't tell Thomas to go visit the empty tomb; He invites him to look at His scars. A tomb points to where you've been, while a scar has the potential to point to where you're going.

So much doubt still exists in us and those around us because we're so busy hiding and covering and running from our scars and our wounds, the very things that made us who we are today. The reason so many of our wounds don't carry the power to transform us is because they failed to include three key elements found in initiation: invitation, transition, and integration. We don't just see it in the man Jesus, we see it in the Old Testament rituals around circumcision given to Abraham. Another intentional marking, only for men, that brought them into pain and allowed them to symbolically experience death in the most sensitive part of what had defined their masculinity. In that ancient tradition, men learned of death's lack of final power and were welcomed to participate in something bigger than themselves.

You may have received the testing, as well as the wounds to prove it, but something will be missing if you were not invited by men with experience and kindness toward you. We may have the elderly around us, but there are very few *elders*, and there's a big difference. Age doesn't always mean you have something to offer. Age only deserves honor if that age carries with it stories of overcoming and the courage to call young men up into a way of living that pushes against the culture they are being seduced to conform to. True elders stand the test of time and maintain an unwavering devotion to Jesus Christ. I'm sorry, but I don't want the advice of an older man whose life was marked by compromise, regardless of how big his platform was or how great his influence appeared. I want to learn from aging men who are walking in purity, in the fullness of their identity, manifesting true humility and courageous kindness. Elders who offer invitation into relationship, not demanding devotion from a pulpit.

That invitation should be into a sacred space, a place of liminality and transition that offers a young man perspective and opportunity to do the work necessary to become who he was uniquely created to become. Within that space, the elders tell story and myth, and explore the intersection between the spiritual and natural worlds while giving young men tools to do the same. They invite them to step out into places that will stretch them, and they walk them to places where they still need to die in order to see resurrection in the places they always wanted to live. They allow young men to be crucified in the areas they need it most, and they don't take them off their cross while they are in the middle of their process.

This process will be difficult for a season. It will require sacrifice, and we will experience a degree of suffering. Wise elders know this and invite us into it, and then they stay with us all the way to the end.

When we've finally learned what we needed to learn, and we've been marked by the experience, we experience what is called integration both in us and around us. It is a return to home, to community, and to a deep sense of purpose within that community. Most of us have never been able to experience the beauty of a moment like this. We were sent out, but we were never able to come back home, and if we did return, it was conditional. I know that *home* can mean a lot of things, but I want to keep it focused on our family of origin and our parents, our primary caregivers, who sent us into the world to school, to jobs, to sports teams, to daycare, and who never knew how to engage with what we experienced out there when they weren't around to guide us. Many of our parents never choose to engage with what truths or lies we picked up along the way about ourselves, the world, relationships, and so much more. It is essential to integration that we give our initiatory experience a place to land with people that see us and can receive us.

Being welcomed home after a formative initiatory experience is one of the most powerful parts of the process, and so many young men are denied it. To return home, and to be engaged with there, becomes the invitation to explore further, to ask bigger questions, and to find greater depth. Regardless of the cost, you know your journey will be worth it because you can return home, and that return gives you the courage to believe that each challenge ahead will provide more opportunity for wisdom, resources, and connection to God, those you love, and the world around you.

Trapped in a Comfort Zone

Men at a deep soul level know these things to be true, so they are calling out to be challenged. When they are not challenged, they challenge themselves, becoming competitive and aggressive. Or some men whose backgrounds were more destructive give in to varying degrees of depression. Grown men and many young boys are trapped in a comfort zone where the highest value is conformity, and everyone is trying to make them feel better, sit still, and not ask too many questions. Men are begging pastors and leaders to invite them into something bigger than themselves, an adventure with spiritual, physical, and psychological depth, an adventure that costs them something. That's why they're showing up at church. They don't just need the songs or sermons; they're longing for an encounter so big it just might kill them! And if it does, they will fade away in the glory of joyful mysticism rather than religious duty.

Instead, men are just invited to the same Bible studies, to reading the same books, to confessing looking at pornography and showing up again the next week to do the same. When men are more aroused by images on their phones and computers than by the women and the world around them, it doesn't necessarily mean they're addicted. It could potentially mean they're bored. Life is no longer providing them with the adventure they know they were made for, so they distract themselves with fantasy. We do the same in grandiose daydreams about power and wealth, choosing to chase the imagery of what "could be" over enaging in the reality of what we have and where we are.

In that vacuum, the depression or aggression grows. Depression makes demands of those around us, wanting them to fill the void of our low self-worth and fulfill all our emotional needs (which drains everyone it encounters). Aggression pushes everyone away through anger and frustrated outbursts (probably while telling others the aggressive person really wants to be close). In both cases, we blame others and make our actions about someone else—something outside ourselves. When the truth is that it's something inside of us that's causing the issues. We are responsible for our thoughts and actions; blame will never get us the transformation we are seeking.

The saddest part of all this is that the men struggling the most are some of the best servants in the Church. The men caught in the most oppressive cycles of porn, the deepest bouts of depression, and the most aggressive behavior are the guys leading and serving on a Sunday. Then those same men, in order to minimize the sting of their transgression, serve more and develop a high degree of Christian moralism put on full display for all to see, which allows them to say with confidence, "I'm not as bad as that guy over there." We develop moral superiority toward others as a defense mechanism to protect our secrets, while forcing out love and any form of accountability.

Some men will even double down on religious fanaticism as a substitute for true encounter, because they can't bear the thought that they might be exposed. To be exposed is the first step toward vulnerability, which is the first step toward authenticity, which is the first step toward true and lasting authority. But the cost for most men is too high. They refuse to yield to the process, to face the giant, take responsibility for their own lives and their own actions, and then see what happens when they step inside the fiery furnace, stand against the crowd, march from King Arthur's court toward the Red Knight with just a little javelin they made back in the forest. In their refusal, they remain in immature boyhood relatively comfortable until they are willing to pay whatever price necessary to move forward in their story.

Uncaging the "Wild Man" Within

Every man of any age who boldly and courageously determines to take those first few steps lays the groundwork for transformation in his life, for something new to happen, for something wonderful and powerful to encounter him not in his strength, but in his weakness. You know what's being asked of you, but can you sacrifice and endure with unwavering determination to cross that threshold? Or will you reject mystery and tension, beauty and the transcendent, in favor of a false initiation based on order and conformity to theological standards, objective truths, and ultimately the opinions of those in charge? Will you stay in the place where the "initiated" are simply the ones who parrot the best and perform well, regardless of what their soul looks like or what their life looks like behind closed doors?

This kind of scenario is of no interest to men who want to experience true transformation. They want to let out the "wild man" inside them who has been caged and oppressed since their youth. This image coined by Robert Bly in his famous book *Iron John* is not about becoming wild, but about finding the part of you that refuses to be a victim to circumstances, the part that is able to own the entirety of your story and take full responsibility for all aspects of it. When this part of us is released from oppression, it scares those in positions of authority and power around us because it demonstrates that we don't need their approval and permission to be who we are and we refuse to fit into their boxes.

When you are able to fully engage with the wild man within you, you might be blamed for being too honest, too connected

110

to your emotions and your story. You no longer live for others' opinions about you. This isn't rebellious; it's freeing. And the proof is that it's done with humility and kindness, not judgment, bitterness, or criticism. Some men become feral as they search for the wild man within. They partner with their aggression and primal instincts in such a way that they need to prove their masculinity through stereotypical feats of strength, endurance, drinking and smoking excessively, dominating women, and defining their identity and success through how much money they make and how many possessions they own. None of this makes you a free wild man; it's a clear sign that you're still a boy. The wild man is still locked inside, buried somewhere in your pain, longing to be let out. More structure, more order, and more systems won't make a way for him; they will bury him further in your psyche, drowning in fear that someone might find out who you really are, including you.

All of this is taking place while the world around us demands that we need more conformity, more order, or we will be left to chaos. Yet the opposite of conformity isn't chaos; it's creativity. We've attempted to standardize everything within the Church in some industrialized fashion, hoping it will transform the world. But classrooms alone don't make disciples, and doctrines diminish deity. Men who can only repeat verses and go on hunting trips for a weekend aren't initiated; they're trapped.

In the story of Iron John, the Wild Man is the one who carries the young prince into the wilderness as he leaves his parent's castle and the safety and security of the life he has known. It is the beginning of the youth's journey into maturity, into initiation, into the renewing of his mind and the transformation he was destined for. Oh, to ride into the beginning of our journey on the shoulders of the wild man we have forgotten and abandoned, so that we could engage the parts of us that make us who we are—parts we've so often rejected because that's

111

what others have taught us to do with the truest parts of our story.

So few men have had the privilege of an initiatory experience that ushered them into their manhood with encouragement and strength. Almost no men I've had the privilege to work with have experienced anything like this. Sometimes I feel as if I want it for them more than they want it for themselves. They are running in circles, tired from all their attempts, and they have no idea what to do next. So they simply give up and decide to do nothing. But what if we were able to rekindle our courage, reignite the divine spark within us, and get pointed in the right direction so that we know what to fight and we could stop fighting ourselves? Maybe it's time to pick a fight—whether you win or lose, at least you know you're alive!

▼ ▼ ▼

Parzival left to claim what he believed was his. He went back out to the meadow, informed Ithir of the knights' collective reluctance to fight him, and claimed that Ithir's armor was his by King Arthur's decree and that Ithir should hand it over willingly or suffer the consequences. Ithir didn't want to fight such an unworthy opponent and stain his reputation, but Parzival took a swipe at him while he was busy looking upon the youth with disdain.

Enraged and insulted, Ithir knocked him back with a kick from his boot so fierce that Parzival was laid upon the grass, with the wind sucked from his chest. Yet his youth was a gift, and he quickly arose from the earth with his small javelin in hand. As he got back into a defensive position, he spied a slit in Ithir's helmet and quickly and accurately flung his javelin through the slit, into Ithir's eye and out the back of his head.

This was considered an unchivalrous act, defeating an opponent with a weapon made for hunting rather than combat. Parzival's javelin was the same weapon he had used in the forest all those years, tracking and gathering small prey for his mother's table. All those who witnessed this ruthless act gasped at the outcome, but Parzival paid no attention, nor did he even know there was any issue. While Ithir lay dying, Parzival began pulling the armor from his body, dragging it around in an unfit display of immaturity and cruelty. This was not Camelot's or King Arthur's way.

It should be noted at this point in the story that Parzival never kills again. This would be his one moment of blatant brutality, done in immaturity—careless and selfish, but not calculated and cruel.

A squire was sent to stop this display and remove the armor for Parzival. As he attempted to dress him in the stunning red armor, the young squire pulled at the tunic Parzival's mother had made for him. Immediately, Parzival exclaimed that nothing of his mother's would ever leave his body. So the new armor was placed over his mother's sackcloth.

Parzival was now on his way to a life of chivalry. He gave his donkey to the squire and mounted the Red Knight's steed, which swelled with power underneath his youthful frame. Then the squire handed him a great lance, placed a sword in the sheath at his side, and put the stunning shield on his back.

As Parzival rode off, he could barely hold on to the raw strength of the horse, which moved at full stride all day, a pace an experienced horseman would have struggled to keep up with. But the problem wasn't in the going; it was in the fact that Parzival had not been trained in stopping. The horse ran until both man and beast were completely worn out.

Parzival didn't return to the court of King Arthur, the castle, or the Round Table, which left a longing in Arthur to find the young prince, to find his strength and courage. There was something inside Arthur that wanted to be near it himself.

▼ ▼ ▼

It is at this point that young Parzival exits adolescence and enters the world of manhood, leaving a mess behind him that others will have to clean up. The cup Ithir took from Arthur's table was returned to the king, and a quest was begun when

113

Parzival possessed the Red Knight's armor, a symbol of engaging with and embracing our aggression, our fearlessness, our courage. We do this all while, as storyteller Martin Shaw would say, "riding on the energy of another man's horse,"[2] since we don't possess the actual courage yet ourselves. This destructive power must be harnessed, not repressed. It must be experienced, wrestled with, and tempered if we are to use it for the benefit of others and defend that which we claim to love.

Parzival begins his move from boyhood to manhood through a violent act of immaturity against an honored and revered masculine figure. The knights of Arthur's own table would not come against the Red Knight because he was both feared and loved. But this is what wounded young men do. They allow their unrestrained egos to drive them to want to defeat publicly those who are in authority over them. In their minds, it proves how strong they are and how worthy they are of masculinity—but above all, it lets those around them know that they were not hurt by the absence or lack of attention given by their father.

This is not the heart of initiation. Initiation is not *against* something; it is always *for* something. When Parzival commits murder, it wasn't primarily about the Red Knight. This brutal act was symbolically against the father Parzival had never known. It was the first time in his young life that he was able to access all that aggression and point it somewhere, even if he couldn't recognize it at the time. So he found a small space between the knight's visor and helmet, a void where he could throw his javelin—a picture of the absent father where he pointed all his violence, all his rage, all his frustration.

We can immediately see in this the cyclical nature of abandonment and violence, of absent fathers and aggressive sons. Is an act like Parzival's catalytic? Yes. Does it move our story forward? Yes. But we have no idea of the cost at this point and that there might be a better way.

So many young boys leave their own homes in the same kind of immature, violent rage. They leave a wake of devastation behind them, thinking they're moving into their manhood, when really they're just avoiding their pain, wearing the disguise of a man without ever becoming one. But that pain, that longing inside them for a father, doesn't disappear. It's just driven deeper and deeper inside so they no longer have to look at it. It doesn't end with their own father either. They do this to any father figure who shows up in their lives. Whether it's a teacher or a pastor or a leader or a boss, their woundedness convinces them that this father figure is something to defeat, not learn from. And many of them prove that true by attempting to manipulate or control them as young men instead of mentoring them.

What young boys need is someone they can contend with and bring their aggression to who can contain it for them without attempting to define it for them. Young men need fathers and mentors who will hear them, hear their pain, frustration, and brokenness, and give them a space for expression without cheap answers or quick fixes; this is the difference between containment and control. What so many insecure fathers and leaders do is point their own aggression back at young men or even peers they feel challenged by, leaving so many men more confused and alone than ever. We end up with millions of men who have never been initiated, and a culture full of men who now worship at the altar of youth because they were denied their own childhood initiatory experience in exchange for entertainment. Entertainment will always be a cheap substitute for encounter. That's why the world spends billions of dollars every year to keep us addicted to the false lights found on movie screens, TV screens, computer screens, and the screens we carry around every day on our phones. Many men would rather live in the fantasy provided by false light so that they never leave it for the true light found only in the holy and the sacred. To leave behind the false light of fantasy and embrace the eternal light we long for requires courage, character, and conviction formed in the fires of initiation so that we can aggressively pursue that which we were always meant to become.

Two Central Questions

Classic initiation practices have always attempted to answer two central questions that are seemingly at play here in this portion of our story, being asked inside each man as he transitions from boyhood to manhood. These two questions are

1. *What do I do with my pain?*
2. *Who will hold my crown until I am big enough to wear it?*

Question 1 reminds us that our pain must be placed somewhere, expressed in some way, or else it will be repressed and form into anxiety, bitterness, or frustration that could show up later as anger. Is this not what we see in the story of Parzival and in so many young men today? They find that small opening and point everything at it that hurts, in a vain attempt to release in rage what could be cared for in rest. Young boys wounded by their adolescent abandonments and unfulfilled childhood longings are left to figure out violent and destructive ways to cope with their experiences, which only drives the pain deeper. The violence doesn't even have to take outward forms toward others; it can be inward, with pessimistic self-talk and a negative self-image continually repeating internally the things watched and heard externally. But the pain doesn't disappear.

There is no version of our lives that allows this first question to go unanswered. It's easy to spot a man's avoidance of it. When asked a deep question that might start to invade his avoidance, he has two answers: "It's no big deal" and "I'm fine." This is a clear sign that you are not fine, and it most definitely is a big deal. Those feelings of avoidance cause anxiety because we don't know what to do with all that pain. With no tools to help, we can easily find ourselves frustrated with ourselves and others.

I think it's also worthwhile to note again that this is the only time Parzival kills in the whole story. It's as if he recognized after the fact that this was not the right way and that moving forward he would do things differently. Then we have to also ask ourselves, *How many people will I kill, reject, or hurt until I attempt to find another way?*

Question 2, an obvious illustration, reminds us that every young boy is born with a crown too big for his head. As we saw in chapter 3, this crown represents who he truly is, his divine potential, and his unique destiny. He spends his young life looking for someone who will hold it for him and help him understand what it's for, so that one day he will be able to wear it with courage and confidence. There is a king in all of us, in the image of the One who created us. The king in us is meant to stand with conviction, courage, and simple devotion to the life we have been given, and with fidelity to the story we are living. A king is the influential authority who creates safety in an environment and reminds all under his care that they are safe to be who they were meant to be.

We have rarely seen men like this. Most men never make it to king, so they remain entitled young princes. Regardless of our experience, we were created to become something more. This becomes even more difficult in the culture we currently inhabit. Today's culture says "youth is king," so young boys are running around thinking they have need of no one. That leaves us with grown men attempting to dress like, sound like, and act like teenagers in order to stabilize their own insecurity by remaining relevant or pseudo-influential. They are as lost and broken as the culture they are attempting to emulate.

This happens both in the Church and in culture. Advertisers and the media work tirelessly to gain the youths' affection and devotion, whoring themselves out to whatever is in fashion in order to manipulate masses by staying ahead of cultural trends, or creating them if necessary. We have no honor for elders and fathers, because they have consistently disappointed and abandoned us. Leaders and pastors and politicians fall, and the youth post and tweet about it, convinced in their immaturity that it all proves they are right and anyone over the age of thirty should never be trusted. When we value youth in this way and demean the wisdom of old age and experience found in wise elders, we in turn devalue true masculinity and what it can offer our sons. We are left with boys still looking for fathers, for mentors, for someone who can hold their crown until they can grow into it themselves.

Gaining Perspective

We need to take the initiative to intentionally seek *something bigger* and *someone better* than we are currently being offered so we can answer these two central questions. This is what true spirituality is attempting to do for us in the form of eternity and in the life of Jesus. Eternity is not an amount of time; it's a place. It's what we call "the Kingdom." This is what Jesus was sharing with us throughout His short life on earth: "the kingdom of heaven is at hand" (Matthew 4:17). It's here; it's now. It's not somewhere you go one day when you die, but somewhere you have the ability to enter into in this life, today.

Eternity offers us perspective on our pain in a way that nothing else can, because it pulls us outside of our current circumstances and our "momentary, light affliction" (2 Corinthians

4:17 NASB), allowing us to receive what we really need in moments of deep suffering—hope. We don't need our pain to be fixed or figured out; we need something more than oversimplistic theological answers "as we look not to the things that are seen but to the things that are unseen" (2 Corinthians 4:18). We need hope!

Perspective gives us hope that our pain has a purpose and that its purpose will give way to the promises we have in our life as we yield to what the pain is teaching us and calling us to pay attention to. Pain points to something we need to address. It's one of the most powerful teachers in our life. The proof is that we all have learned the most in the most difficult and painful seasons of our lives, if we've been willing to give pain's lessons our attention. Pain in connection to eternal perspective teaches us that regardless of how long it takes, this heartache, this loss, this frustration will give way to something deeper, if we don't quit (Galatians 6:9). That's how you learn, how you get stronger, how you grow in any area of life—don't quit.

But it's not just my pain. What do I do with this purpose, this crown I was given when I entered this life as a young boy? What do I do with all this potential inside me that I fully embraced back when I was young and didn't know any better? Maybe your crown was stolen from you. Maybe you gave it to the wrong person to hold and you still haven't figured out how to get it back. I offer you this: Jesus is the only one big enough to hold your crown, because He was the one who gave it to you in the first place.

Of course, we are meant to have older men in our lives who represent Jesus on earth, who carry His heart in an attempt to care for us. But our eyes, our hearts have to be fixed on Him alone. Despite how many times we've been let down and disappointed, He is the one who remains the same yesterday, today, and forever—another picture that He is not only offering us eternity, but that He is eternity itself, our eternal Father in Heaven.

I need the training of men who have walked this road before me. I need a father, someone who unselfishly, without control and manipulation, can see my God-given potential and help me make sure I don't forget it in seasons of life where I might not be able to see it for myself anymore. When the pain becomes too much to bear, or the sumptuous distractions of the world lure me in a direction other than where I was meant to go, these elders call me home.

This is initiation.

You cannot initiate yourself, and you cannot be initiated by your peers. A true initiatory experience begins when wise elders invite us to leave business as usual, enter a sacred space of transition where we can wrestle with our pain, our sorrow, and our anger in ways that allow us to fully integrate who we are with where we have been. We do not do this just for ourselves but for the benefit of others within our tribes, our communities, and our families. Our pain offers us perspective, and the potential of who we could become is cared for and covered by those who see us and are pushing us into the fullness of what we were created for.

You may not have received this kind of care and connection in your life, but that doesn't mean you can't find it. The work is hard, but it is possible, if you are willing to put one foot in front of the other.

THE WORK

In order to temper male aggression, we must begin to wrestle with the reality of our story, our experiences, the highs and lows that come with our trauma and triumphs. As we do this, we can let go of the anger, the frustration, the bitterness, and in some cases rage, as well as the anxiety and depression that that can develop because we haven't done the work necessary to understand how we ended up where we are today. You can begin this process by mapping your own story. In appendix III, you will find what we call "The Story Map," a simple way of charting how you got to where you are and the experiences that formed you into the man you are today, from care and connection to sexuality and faith. You can find different versions of this tool. One version is Jon Tyson's "Mountains and Valleys," which he refers to in his training course for fathers called "The Primal Path." This found its origin in Viktor Frankl's work called the "Mountain Range Exercise," which he used as a tool in the form of psychology he developed called logotherapy. There is also a version you can search for called a "Life Map," which exists in many different forms. You can look into all these versions and more, but right now, appendix III will be a good place to start. This is my attempt at providing a similar tool to help you name parts of your story that you may have previously passed over.

Developing a story map of your own will allow you to obtain some perspective on the moments in your life that have defined you the most—not just the broken parts, but the beautiful parts as well. We will do more with this tool in later chapters, but this is the place to begin. As you start, ask yourself two main questions: *When did I cross from boyhood to manhood?* and *What happened to my crown?* Your story map will help you answer these questions. Look at the tool and instructions in appendix III and see what you are able to uncover in four key areas: family of origin, faith, relationships (friends and romantic), and sexuality.

Path 7

Finding a Wise Elder

A baronial king entered, accompanied in procession by many attendants. He walked up to the young groom and embraced him. The guest said, "I am Iron John, who through an enchantment became turned into a Wild Man. You have freed me from the enchantment. All the treasure that I own will from now on belong to you."

—Robert Bly, *Iron John: A Book about Men*

I must confess that this is a hard chapter to write.

I don't want to seem overly cynical, but it seems to me that as I've journeyed through my own story, I've consistently been let down by those in leadership, both within the walls of the Church and beyond. Everything goes well as long as I am performing well, staying within the boundaries of the particular church culture I'm involved with, toeing the line between what I feel and what's being presented, never asking too many questions. But if you question convention, disagree with the way things are handled, or choose to step outside church protocol, you will be pushed back into line or forced out completely. It doesn't matter how much your life or your gifts have impacted the community, transformed lives, or shaped the current culture. If you don't fit in, you will probably be asked to move on.

I simply want to be transparent and let you know that I have wounds here and that I'm still processing the effect this has had on me. They're not open wounds; they have become scars upon the skin of my journey of faith that I am proud to wear. I am also willing to discuss them with those who have had similar experiences and have yet to find peace with that, who don't want to allow it to shape the way they view God or respond to His people. We cannot allow our pain to affect someone else's process. We need the Church. We need its beautiful and multifaceted expression to reach as many people with the love of Jesus as possible. But we have to accept that people who are hurting, hurt other people. That those who have done damage to others with their positions are doing so because they've been unwilling to do the work we're addressing within the pages of this book.

We are living in a culture that desires to expose all those who have done wrong as if it's something new. Entire documentaries and podcast series are done on dysfunctional leaders and the people impacted by their influence. But this has been happening in humanity way before churches were founded, and we see it in the Biblical text in stories about men who were clearly utilized by God for His purposes on earth. I mean, Abraham is sleeping with his wife's servant, Moses is getting drunk, clearly Saul had some large and undeniable internal struggles, David is sleeping with another man's wife and having him killed, all while being a pretty awful father. And we can continue this discourse by walking through the Old Testament books of Kings and Chronicles and making a list of individuals God had apparently chosen who had a litany of psychological and spiritual issues. That doesn't even get us caught up to Judas in the New Testament. This is an old story with modern themes. We just have much larger communication platforms that allow for an entire generation to witness people's downfalls while they're still in process.

Yet some of those same people I just mentioned from Scripture, along with many others of questionable backgrounds, are found in Hebrews 11, which has become known as the Hall of Faith. I'm not making excuses or justifying leaders' poor behavior, abuses, or blatant manipulation of those they lead. What I want us to see is that we can choose to blame them and then identify as victims, but that will only lead us to greater and greater victimizations because things go from something that happened to me, to something I am. And anything we identify with, we believe we deserve.

Breaking the Cycle

If we want to break the cycle of victimization in our lives and help expose the cycle to others, we have to separate who we are from the hurt we have experienced. This gives us perspective on our pain and allows us to utilize it in the progression of our journey, rather than letting it limit us or withhold us from reaching our full potential. If we stop growing, stop doing the work, we allow victimization to continue having its hold on us and giving us valid reasons for bailing on the idea of wise elders all together, never wanting to trust again, never wanting to risk again, and in many cases never wanting to love again.

For men, this can take a dark turn. They use their hurt from others as a reason to dominate and control those within their sphere of influence. This not only continues the cycle of pain, but it allows them to no longer feel like a victim. In the process of burying their own experiences, they never realize that they have become the thing that hurt them. We must look at our hurt, wrestle with it, and process it with other men, lest we never reach our full potential in Christ and give up our power because of how someone else chose to use theirs. We must learn to utilize the wrongs done to us by others as fuel to become something more than we were offered, not an excuse to reject who we were meant to become.

In the story of Iron John, he begins as an ugly beast of a man found at the bottom of a pond, covered in red, wiry hair from the top of his head down to his toes. But at the end of our story, he arrives looking entirely different at the wedding of the young prince and his new bride. Spoiler warning: He arrives as a king who has been delivered from an enchantment, originally placed on him for reasons the story never tells. He had been living a cursed life ever since, but now he reenters the story in his restored body, handsome and strong, displaying his wealth and power, surrounded by a procession of attendants, and declaring that all he has is now the young prince's.

What happened? Why the change? Why the great display of generosity? When the young prince embraced his story, made the necessary sacrifices in all the right ways, and came into his fullness, the enchantment was broken on Iron John, the one who first led him. There is a cyclical nature to this experience that we can see in many stories and possibly in our own lives. We have the ability to bring healing to those individuals who first helped us. When we first meet him in the story, Iron John is in the forest, devouring hunters. Then because of the young prince, he returns to who he was meant to be.

Have you ever seen the movie *Whiplash*? It's the same in that story. The mentor, attempting to embarrass and destroy a beautiful opportunity for a young apprentice, is found in disbelief when instead of being embarrassed, the boy seizes the moment. He doesn't crumble and retreat; he leans into his identity and his gifts, creating something beautiful out of a devastating situation. The mentor is stunned in the process and transforms into the boy's biggest supporter.

We may have experienced mentors who, in their own brokenness, mishandled our gifts and our hearts. They may have demeaned our efforts and manipulated our opportunities in order to benefit themselves, all because of pain and hurt we never get to hear about. It is only when we overcome these obstacles and step into who we were meant to become that their stories are complete. They become who they were meant to become, all because we didn't quit.

One Continuous Lineage of Devotion

"You intended to harm me, but God intended it for good," declares Joseph from the book of Genesis (Genesis 50:20 NIV). We also find this kind of scenario in the final section of the Hebrews 11 faith chapter: "And all these, though commended through their faith, did not receive what was promised, since God had provided something better for us, that apart from us they should not be made perfect" (verses 39–40). Their story isn't finished until you and I come into the fullness of our story.

That's how God set it up. Generations serving one another, uniting us throughout history in one continuous lineage of devotion that allows the generation behind us to pick up where we left off as an inheritance that cannot be stolen and is impervious to inflation rates, governmental shifts, and the cost of real estate or the price of bread. We must become the mentors we never had. When you cannot find the thing you are looking for in the people you're surrounded with, it might be a sign that you are supposed to become it.

▼ ▼ ▼

That evening, exhausted from their journey, horse and rider came upon another castle. Sitting under a lime tree near the entrance was its owner, Gurnemanz, with gray hair and aging body. He immediately saw that Parzival's stance was not that of a warrior—slumped over on his steed, shield dangling over his shoulder like a half-dead goose. He took interest in this young boy the evening breeze had just blown in.

Remembering his mother's advice, Parzival was quick to recognize the gray hair of Gurnemanz and ask him for advice in exchange for his service. Gurnemanz recognized something of himself in the boy and invited him in.

Pages quickly appeared and bathed and clothed Parzival for bed. That night, he slept soundly and quite deeply, more deeply than he could ever remember in his whole life. The following morning, he was introduced to the castle, as well as to several knights training on the grounds. They all recognized something of nobility in him, something that rode alongside his lack of experience.

Gurnemanz asked him of his journey, and Parzival gave him the details of the great quest he had recently begun. The old man groaned at the death of the Red Knight, but from then on only referred to Parzival with that title. Then at a break in the conversation, an irritated Gurnemanz spoke up: "Why is it that you keep going on about your mother's advice? If you really want to learn something, allow *me* to give you a few bits of advice."

First, Gurnemanz told Parzival a few of his experiences concerning the feminine. He advised, "Never seduce or be seduced by a woman. Also, never forsake the cause of a woman." He added, "Seek noble and loyal love so you will never find disgrace, and so the love you find will never part from you, come what may."

Then he spoke to Parzival as a knight: "In all your courage and all your fierceness, you must remember mercy."

Finally, Gurnemanz offered him the most dangerous advice he would receive: "Never ask too many questions. Be silent in the presence of greatness and glory." On the road ahead, in another season and another

castle, this one piece of advice would leave Parzival lost and alone, clinging to darkness, frustrated with God Himself as he attempted to find
what all of this could mean.

But for now, Parzival was in the castle of a godfather, a mentor who
would train the young boy in the ways of manhood and chivalry.

▼ ▼ ▼

This is another scene where Parzival is offered a perverted
knot of advice he would later have to untangle. One piece is
more destructive than the others: "Never ask too many questions." Asking questions is a key component to sustaining our
growth, especially if we are asking those questions of men
wiser and more experienced than we are. Yet we live in a culture of uninitiated, insecure men who have found their way
into positions of leadership within the educational system, the
government, business, and yes, even the Church. Within each
of these structures, they are doling out the same destructive
advice, unable, in their woundedness, to see the error of their
ways. The damaging consequence of this bad advice is that we
never ask the necessary questions of those who have gone before us, and we therefore end up building foundations for living
and leading that hinder us from ever reaching our God-given
potential.

This wounded instruction not only determines how we act
when we are in the presence of true wisdom and experience; it
also lays the foundation for how we believe we should be treated
once we are in a position of authority. This creates cycles of
bondage to systems that tell us "Here's the answer," "Don't
ask questions," "You don't understand," and finally, "Trust
me." When people in your environment or under your leadership aren't allowed to question your authority, they are not
submitted; they're slaves. And the men who kick back against
these systems aren't rebellious; they are courageous—when it's

done with humility and mercy, not another distorted version of control and manipulation.

Going Soul Deep and Heaven High

Remember, if your goal is to be right, you are already wrong. No quest, no transformation can begin without knowing the right question to ask or what question we are attempting to answer. The simple advice not to ask questions may keep you in the good graces of those in power and could possibly give you the appearance of authority and influence. However, the exchange is that you won't have the opportunity for growth and development that you would under a healthy, mature mentor.

This way of thinking was introduced to the Church in the 1970s, during what became known as the Shepherding movement. This movement coined phrases like "spiritual fathers and mothers" and "spiritual covering" that are now commonplace in a charismatic church culture. These phrases all came from five men, the "Fort Lauderdale Five," who banded together following the moral failures of major charismatic church leaders in the Florida area. The movement was a reactionary response to these men's disappointment in other people's inability to maintain character, not a heartfelt response to the needs of the communities they were leading. In the movement's peak, there were over one hundred thousand people submitted to what they considered to be godly leadership and accountability structures. But it was all fear based, and the right questions went unasked. I believe it laid a lot of the foundation for the men's gatherings we experience today that shame men into submission so they know how sinful they are, but never show them how powerful they are.

We're afraid of men's sin more than we're in awe of who they could become. This will always lead to abuses in power, and to immature men willing to yield to these structures because they believe it's the only thing that makes them "good." We gather men like this in weekly "accountability groups" and then wonder why men don't move beyond them. In and of themselves, accountability groups and weekend excursions into the forest don't provide the adventure men are longing for. Adventure and the process of initiation are soul deep and heaven high. These require a sacredness and ritual experience led by men who make it their priority to reveal the fullness of who each man could become through the lens of his unique story and the light of eternity, rather than simply revealing his flawed humanity.

Most men don't need another space in their life where they're being told what they're doing wrong. Even sharing it in a group isn't always helpful, because most men know what they're doing wrong. The help they need is someone in their life reminding them of what they're doing right and what's locked inside them that demands to be let out.

If I can identify your struggle but don't have the capability to call you beyond it, then I'm no help to you. The beauty of true mentorship and discipleship relationships is that they mirror your identity and strength back to you through your deepest wounds and the behaviors you still struggle to rectify. True mentorship doesn't see your struggles as issues to overcome, but as symptoms of a deeper lack of understanding of yourself, the wounds you've experienced, and your place within the world you inhabit.

Behavioral change is always about new values, not more accountability. Look at it this way: You don't get skinny by not wanting to be fat. You need a new set of values for healthy eating, for strength, for greater life expectancy, and for feeling good in your own skin. This is what great mentors offer—a picture of possibility that you have yet to see, due to your pain, lack of experience, or shame.

This is why mentorship must always be an invitation, not a demand. If you have to defend your authority or position in someone's life, I'd question whether or not you had it in the first place. The call of Jesus is "Follow Me." There's no force, there's no guilt, there's no "Well, let's see if you can do this. I know you're not ready and you have a lot of personal issues to work through before you can actually do anything of value, but let's start anyway . . ."

Good Godfathers Point to the Father

Discipleship is simple: If you see something of value in who I am, then join me on the journey, and I can take you places in yourself and in God that you didn't even know were possible. Then Jesus takes it a step further and states, "Anyone who has seen me has seen the Father" (John 14:9 NIV). You won't find in Scripture a model for "spiritual fathers and mothers" within the Body of Christ. I do believe that most leaders using this language are not trying to intentionally hurt others, and I know most people mean well. But the message of Jesus is that "you only have one Father" (see Matthew 23:9). All other models and individuals over the course of your lifetime will point to Him, if they offer anything of value.

Don't go looking for another father; you already have one. That's the message of good mentors and godfathers. Locked up inside the aging frame of men who can no longer fight are the knowledge and wisdom of how to fight for the one thing that really matters—love. That's why Gurnemanz dives straight into his advice about women and then mercy. Love manifests in many ways in a man's life, but none greater than his love for God, and that expression of love lived out in his home, with his wife and his kids. This way of living and loving doesn't happen by accident; it's something hard-fought for over many years and decades.

It's this exchange between the generations that allows us to identify our own purpose and pain, without submitting to someone else's prescription of how we are to live that out. We must learn to fight, not to be violent. That was the emphasis of Gurnemanz's wisdom: "In all your courage and all your fierceness, you must remember mercy."

The fight I'm referring to is psychological, emotional, and spiritual. It transforms who we are and therefore how we engage with our life and the people in it. This fight results in a man who knows how to stand steadfast and consistent over the course of time because he knows who he is and what he is capable of. He is not swayed by public opinion or cultural relevance; he stands out with no desire to fit in. He must go to war with the lies he has been taught, the views that limit his potential, and the pain that has defined his actions and reactions. Then, in mercy, he sends them into service in his life as transformed experiences that develop transformed expression.

▼ ▼ ▼

Gurnemanz immediately threw Parzival into the training a young warrior needed. The young man learned how to fight defensively, how to mount a powerful steed well, and how to carry a shield. As he learned jousting and swordplay within the next several weeks, the courtyard was littered with tired knights who could not keep up with the youth's ferocity.

Then every evening, the young warrior and the wise elder sat together by the fire, eating, drinking, and laughing. Parzival listened intently to Gurnemanz as he shared stories of his life. This was where Parzival learned that Gurnemanz had already lost three sons in battle, and this was the great pain of the elder's life. It was why secretly he desired that young Parzival would stay and marry his daughter, Laize, who had been waiting on them each evening, preparing their meals for what had now turned into months of time together. And it was not just her father, but also Laize herself who had fallen for Parzival.

Parzival, however, began to think on his mother and wonder how she was. Everything he ever wanted was laid out right in front of him—he could have a wise mentor, a beautiful bride, a wonderful castle. Surely he could have it all, if he stayed. But he longed to see his mother again, and the ache in his heart only grew and brought a cloud over his time within the walls of Gurnemanz's castle. So Parzival determined he would leave and return home.

It was a horrible scene for Gurnemanz as he rode with Parzival to the edge of the kingdom. He watched the ghosts of three sons ride off with the youth.

For the first time, Parzival felt conflict in his heart. He wanted to stay, yet he wanted to know what had become of his mother. The farther he rode, the more conflicted he became. He yielded to the strength of the steed and allowed it to lead him. His conflict, confusion, and grief built with each stride toward his destination. The horse sped past familiar landscapes, charging forward until it reached the coast. The smell of salt in the air seemed to lighten Parzival slightly, to bring clarity back to his mind. He grasped onto it, even if it was but a mist within his mind, and he found a small space for peace to reside there.

This short vision was shattered by noise coming from across the bay. In the distance he saw another castle, surrounded by warriors, clearly under attack. His peace would have to wait. A warrior was needed, and a quest was still at hand.

▼ ▼ ▼

We are searching for a man who will help us steward our gifts and the power we know we possess. He must be a man who has walked this road before. We want such men's stories; we want their experiences for ourselves. They have been to places and seen things that our earthly fathers have not. This longing to learn from such men causes us to want to stay under their influence for as long as possible. Yet it also drives us out into the world, to know more and experience more because they introduce us to opportunities we didn't even know were available to us and our fathers didn't know how to offer us.

This is actually a beautiful thing, not a bad thing. Men need other men to continue the work of initiation in their sons in ways that they themselves cannot. Tribes did this naturally, but now we must do it intentionally, pulling together the resources we have through relationships to introduce our sons to experiences we don't have access to ourselves. Who around you can bring positive impact and new perspective to your son? What athletes, what occupations, what finances? Do you know someone who can teach young men to fish, to camp, to build, to work on cars, to learn an instrument? Gurnemanz was such a man for Parzival.

Crying Uncle

In myth, you will sometimes find the phrase "the uncle who lives at the edge of the wilderness." It's a way of saying someone who lives in the tension between the security of the village and the untamed potential of the wilderness. It was a scary place where the unexpected could happen, and often did. This uncle is the one families would send their young boys to in the midst of the boys' initiation process.

In one such story, a young boy is acting rebelliously, getting into all sorts of trouble, hanging out with the wrong crowd. His parents finally say, "Enough is enough. We're sending you to your uncle."

The boy responds with fear and offers to compromise. He demands another option, but the choice is made and the boy is sent. When he arrives, the uncle, hairy and disheveled but keen-eyed and focused, says "You will go into the forest every day—"

The boy cuts the uncle off with his excitement: "I know I can I be a great hunter! I can hunt rabbit and deer and fox and bear. I'll bring game back, and we'll feast. Train me. Let's do this! I'm ready to begin."

But the uncle just stares, and the boy instantly recognizes he has made a grievous mistake. The uncle says, "You will go into the forest each day and find an oak to befriend, and you will sit beneath it in silence. Then you will come back to me and tell me what you have observed." The boy's shoulders slump down in disappointment. The uncle continues, "You will do this for five years."

This is a powerful story, one rich with symbolism and complexity. You won't find a simple five-point strategy for initiating your son or having him become a better man within the walls of the uncle's house. This is wilderness wisdom only found in a man who has been through some pain and has lived to tell the tale. Most of our experiences have been sterilized and distilled to make it palatable for others to receive, but this is a deeper invitation, one given by a wise elder who isn't interested in wasting our time or playing childish games. If you want transformation, you have to be ready to do the hard work.

The young boy in the story probably had the troublemaking part of his personality passed down to him from his father, but it would be his uncle (probably the father's brother) who knew how to temper it into something useful that would become a resource to the boy over the course of his lifetime. This gives us a new appreciation for the father's lack and the wisdom he showed in sending his boy into service in the wild forest. A good father knows how to pull in other men to offer his son what he cannot. This humility gives the son access to resources that he couldn't otherwise find at home. In tribal communities this was easier. Young boys were able to experience a wide range of masculine energies and perspectives over the course of their young lives as they developed into men. We lack this in our modern experience, so a young boy is left wandering and wanting, while his father is left feeling frustrated by his own limitations.

Without exposure to the masculine world in this way, many young men slowly sink back home into the safe, nurturing care of the feminine. They want coddling instead of correction, and they need the constant affirmation of a woman's voice because they've never heard the confident invitation of an experienced and kind man calling them into courage. These men end up wanting their lovers to be mothers and to care for all their emotional and physical needs, without question or regardless of how they act. The realm of the mother will always distract us from the realm of the mentor. We want her loving embrace, want her to rub our heads and tell us it's all okay. But it's not. You're a grown man, and you have to stop running home to Mommy—especially if you're suffering from a mother wound and your return is just a codependent attempt to make yourself feel okay by making your mom feel okay.

Remember that Parzival in our story is still covered under his armor by his mother's tunic. He has refused to take it off, insisting that "nothing of my mother's will ever leave my body." Even Gurnemanz notices Parzival's devotion to his mother's advice when he's attempting to draw him into the realm of the masculine. Parzival looks like a man on the outside, wears the clothing and has the language, but something is off and everyone around him can recognize it. We must let go of the need for nurturing and learn how to self-soothe, or we will succumb to addictive patterns of behavior in order to compensate for the separation anxiety we wrestle with in being away from our mother's support and care.

A mother's nurturing is completely different than the affection provided by a lover. We move from a mother's embrace to a father's discipline, and then into a lover's embrace. Then we move into the discipline of the masculine—only this time it's our masculinity in an environment of our choosing, to invest ourselves however we will best be in service to those we love, protect, and provide for.

Moving Forward Is a Must

Our story must move forward in this way. We cannot return to the innocence of our youth. It no longer exists. We have killed the Red Knight, and we must grow up. We can touch the child-like joy of our youth, the laughter, and the play. It's healthy to do so, but we're not kids anymore. Any man still sitting in his mother's basement, playing video games, with no commitment to a woman and without a job or a career, simply has not yet done the work necessary to cross into manhood.

This is not an accusation; this is a fact. Regardless of whether or not you are married or have children of your own you must move forward with your life. We, as men, must pursue the fullness we were intended for by getting up and putting one foot in front of the other, most especially when we don't "feel like it." Some men I have worked with think that "moving forward" means they should bail on a job they don't like, a difficult relationship they are in, a hard marriage they can't fix, or rebellious kids who won't listen in the selfish avoidance of difficult circumstances, just so they can start over because they think it will be easier the next time around. It won't, and moreover, you will miss the blessing of long-term commitment and the transforming work of faithfulness beyond your feelings. Again, if you aren't married, this still applies to you, your job, your friends, your commitment to service, and the self-sacrificial foundations of a life lived for others. But we cannot do this alone.

Wise elders will expose us to ourselves, peel back the layers of our vanity, and then walk us to the edge of our experience and theirs, bearing their own sadness. And knowing their own

138

limitations, they will usher us into the next season of our journey. Many churches and ministries I've experienced are building orphanages instead of families as they try to get young men (and women) to *stay* instead of *go.*

I'm not talking about physical orphanages; I'm speaking to the mentality that keeps us dependent on systems and people rather than launching us confidently out into the world. This launching is what families do, and what mentors long to accomplish. The goal is to send you, not keep you. True mothers and fathers want to see a young boy, now a young man, move forward in his story so that his experiences have a lasting impact on himself and the world he explores. There must be a coming and going, and in that experience, you are not just tolerated, you are celebrated.

Mentorship with one individual is not usually lifelong; your life will find new expressions, new teachers, and new resources for development in order for your story to keep moving forward. Parzival isn't deemed "rebellious" for his departure. It's a choice and is neither bad nor good; it simply is. You see the tension in him as he rides away. Sometimes we don't know why we are moving forward; we simply have to do it. No need for religious God language like "the Lord told me." A mature man has no need for scapegoats or escape plans in case it doesn't work out. He owns his decisions, as well as the consequences and blessings that come with them. Whatever happens next, he will learn from it and be better because of it. He knows that he worships a God who wastes nothing.

--------------- THE WORK ---------------

I want you to consider the men you know and make a list of the possible ones who have something to offer you as a man.

These are not peers; don't look for someone in the same stage of life as you. Look for someone more experienced.

Maybe these men you will find are not leaders in the traditional sense. Maybe they are sitting in the back row of church. Or maybe one of them is the guy at work who has been faithful to family, job, and Christ for his lifetime. Maybe it's an uncle or godfather figure in your own family line.

I'm not asking you to make some long-committed relationship with these people. I'm simply saying to start looking around. Get curious and explore this question with intention: *Who are the men around me, and are there any who might be able to offer me wisdom in an area of my life where I want to see growth?*

Write down some names, pray about it, and invite one or more of them to a meal or coffee so you can ask a few questions. The right man will make himself available to you.

Path 8

Encountering Divine Femininity

> So God created man in his own image, in the image of God he created him; male and female He created them. . . . And the man and his wife were both naked and were not ashamed.
>
> —Genesis 1:27; 2:25

When a boy encounters a girl for the first time as someone who is not like him, it is an otherworldly experience. When she is no longer just the playmate or the neighbor, she becomes something else altogether—the attraction, the arousal, the fear, the longing, the utter humiliation when you try to speak to one of these sacred creatures and nothing comes out of your mouth. Then you have your first date, your first kiss, the awkward awakening of sexual desire before you know what to do with it . . . and then hopefully one day you commit your whole life, your whole being to one woman for the rest of your life, for richer, for poorer, in good times and bad, in sickness and in health, until death do you part.

Women are a divine gift to men, both to humble and complete them. This happens as a man and a woman yield to one another for the benefit of something more than they could ever have alone. God in His eternal wisdom made them "male and female" with intention; His design was not random. Men and women are different internally and externally, and the unique design of each has perplexed theologians, philosophers, politicians, and psychiatrists, as well as anyone who has ever been in a relationship.

But the fundamental questions remain the same: "What does it mean to be a man and not a woman?" and "What does it mean to be a woman and not a man?" We all know that they differ emotionally, physically, psychologically, and biologically, but I have yet to rest on an answer complete enough to do justice to the complexity and beauty of these questions. Here's what I do know: God doesn't make mistakes, and He is always intentional. God paid special attention to everything about you and your story—from the day you were born, to the city you were born in, to your family, your personality, and yes, even your gender.

As a boy grows in maturity, he realizes the precious opportunity he has to love and cherish this gift of a woman from God and to serve the divine nature found in his opposite, yet his equal. With so much in common and so much that differs between men and women, a mature man grows to realize that to truly understand God and himself, he must learn to yield some of his strength to one woman, his bride, as she does the same for him. Man and woman, though marked from eternity with the unique image of God upon them, view the world from two wildly mysterious perspectives. The true power of a relationship between them is found in how much there is to explore.

142

Changing the Dance

A man feels both empowered and powerless in a woman's presence, and if he is not too wounded from the journey of his experiences with love and heartbreak, then he will be able to see that in her is an image of God that is not in him. He will be able to see the invitation he has to be a protector and provider of that image, so they can pass along to their children what they carry as a couple. A man fosters this by giving the mother the safety and security required for her to make her children a priority above every other opportunity she may receive.

Children change the dance between a husband and wife. As husband and wife become father and mother, the woman finds herself with the gift to nurture and draw the children into love in ways that the father is unable to do. But he has something else to offer—where the woman draws the children in, he empowers them to go out into a dangerous world with courage and confidence. The mother and father do this dance with honor, yielding to each other's strengths and perspectives for something bigger than being right or wrong.

A strong man doesn't have to make demands of his bride, and a strong woman doesn't have to make demands of her husband. In a submitted and committed relationship, each partner is invited to serve the other, and in doing so, the two find each other and find God.

One gender is not better than the other. One does not control the other. One does not dominate the other. Men and women yield to one another in a dance, not a desperate grabbing for attention, affection, and affirmation. God desires that men and women willingly offer themselves to one another in mutual submission, for the benefit of the greater good. We must depart from independence, which births loneliness, and leave behind codependence, which births bondage, in order to experience the strength of interdependence, which gives birth to connection.

▼ ▼ ▼

As Parzival approached the castle across the bay, he had to lead his horse across a rickety bridge that swayed this way and that in the wind. Weary soldiers told him to turn back, but he paid them no mind. He kept his gaze resolute on the battle that lay in front of him. This caused the other soldiers to fear him as he continued his approach. They thought a man so powerful and unmoved by these dangerous circumstances must have troops following, so they retreated to the castle.

Parzival followed and pounded on the enormous gate that defended the rear of the castle. After some convincing, they allowed him entrance. He was escorted into the great hall. Pageantry and grandiosity gave way to chaos and confusion within that space because of the battle now at hand.

As Parzival approached the throne, he found that the owner of this great castle was not a grizzled old warrior king, but a queen named Condwiramurs, sometimes called Blanchefleur, "the White Flower." The throne had been left to her after the death of her father, with no husband to rule by her side. As he approached the queen, he recognized that there were men of war surrounding them, watching every move. Even the castle's workmen, as well as some of the women, carried weapons. No one seemed to have eaten much in months. They looked half-starved. Deprived of animal fat and the taste of wine, their skin was gray, and their eyes were distracted.

Nothing could have prepared Parzival for the beauty of Condwiramurs.

If the castle of Gurnemanz was the masculine, this was surely the feminine, the inner feminine found in all men. Condwiramurs was the bright center of all Parzival had ever known—the meadow at dawn, the clear pool found in a desert, a vision full of endless exploration and never-ending complexity. Parzival was undone for life.

He sat mute in the presence of this radiance. After a short conversation initiated by the queen, the young man was led into the grandest sleeping chamber he had ever entered. The castle attendants helped him out of his shoes and coverings. "Not my mother's tunic," he said, so it was left on him, under his sleeping robes, as they quietly prepared the room for his slumber.

In the middle of the night, he was awakened by Condwiramurs, drenched in flowing silk lit by the moonlight, her face glittering with tears. Startled by her presence, he offered her a place to sit, and even offered his bed. If she wanted to sleep there herself, he would go sleep elsewhere.

Instead, this beautiful queen said to him, "If you do not seek to conquer me, I would like to come rest beside you."

Their innocence had not yet been turned to lustful desires, so it was that they were able to lie with one another in a kind embrace—desire and purity giving way to holiness. This they were able to recognize and honor, without giving in to anything more.

In the safety of that space, the likes of which she had never known, Condwiramurs told Parzival why the siege was taking place upon her castle. A king from a foreign land was attempting to take her as his bride. He had sent his greatest knight, Kingrun, to claim her and bring her to him. She did not want to marry for duty or land or loyalty, however, but for love alone. She said she would rather drown herself in a moat than give her virginity to a king simply looking to make another claim and conquest. Tomorrow, Kingrun would return. He had already jousted with and killed the greatest warriors in her kingdom. If something was not done, she would surely be taken.

Parzival, stirred by what he heard and by his deep love for Condwiramurs, said he would never allow such a thing to happen. He assured her that all his strength would be at her disposal to vanquish such a foe and to defend her honor and the kingdom she was left to steward.

This moved the queen to greater tears and deeper comfort. They stayed entangled in this moment for the rest of the night. Just before dawn, she left and went back to her chambers before anyone could see that she had been there.

▼ ▼ ▼

Parzival left the castle of Gurnemanz to find his mother, and instead he found a lover. This narrative is familiar to many men, whether they can recognize it or not. The repercussions of such an encounter leave men who can't see it for what it is frustrated by their attempts to turn their lovers into mothers. In vain they try to restore what they didn't receive, or try to repair that which wounded them so deeply.

We see this demonstrated in our story through the name of the beautiful queen Parzival has just encountered, a name that is different in the two main versions of the story. Her name in Chrétien's French version is Blanchefleur, meaning "the white flower," but in Wolfram's German version her name is Condwiramurs, meaning "a guide to love." Blanchefleur is a beautiful depiction of the return to innocence and the value of virginity, but Condwiramurs is something altogether different. Virgin, yes, but she represents an invitation to training as well, in an intimate area most men avoid or abuse over the course of their transition from boyhood to manhood.

Defense, but Not Disneyland

This is how we begin to move from the embrace of a mother to the embrace of a lover—by learning how to defend the heart, mind, and body of our beloved. You cannot stay in the embrace of your mother and fully embrace the heart of a lover. We were created to know the care of a mother who sees our goodness despite our behavior, and who defends the core of who we are as she takes delight in us. This is what a young man is supposed to experience in his first encounters with the feminine through

146

his mother. It's your mom's job to defend you, not the other way around. A mother should look at you in any season and call out who you really are, as long as she still has breath in her lungs. As invaluable as that is, at some point you have to mature into having a mutual caring relationship with your beloved, not just being cared for by your mother.

I remember a moment in high school where I was accused of ditching class, and my mother stepped in. Now, just to be clear, I actually was ditching. The school staff simply didn't have any proof that would allow them to do anything about it. But regardless, the next day they decided to suspend me and were going to call my mom. I told them this would not be a wise choice on their part. Thinking I was attempting to save myself, they called her anyway. What they received was an earful they would not soon forget! My mom let them know that she was on her way to school and that she wanted to see the principal. When she arrived, she demanded proof of their accusations and defended my innocence with vigor and lots of colorful language. When she was told that the principal couldn't see her, she simply burst through the door anyway and gave her a piece of her mind. The principal, also a woman, met her head on. It was a stalemate until my mom said that she wouldn't punish me for the senseless repercussions of the baseless accusations they were throwing at me. She said if they wanted to suspend me, that was fine. She would take me to Disneyland.

Of course, I was thrilled. This was an incredible thing to experience, and now I was going to Disneyland too? We got some paperwork, hastily filled it out, and walked to the car. As soon as we got in, I inquired, "When will we be heading to Disneyland?"

Mom whipped around with fire in her eyes and told me, "You're grounded for the foreseeable future!"

147

The entire time, she knew I had acted wrongly. She knew I deserved to be punished, but she was defending her son, not his actions. She knew who I was, and she wasn't going to let one mistake on my part determine how others would see me or treat me. This is the heart of a mother, the feminine strength and energy needed for a young man to know he is loved and seen for who he is, not just for how he acts.

This is where we need to take some time to grieve the places in our lives where we were not seen by our mother, and begin to let go of the fantasy version of our mother we have created in order to compensate psychologically for pain we've endured. Most of our mothers are not evil creatures intending to do harm; they are simply broken people attempting to love in ways that distorted how we see ourselves and how we experience the feminine in our lives, from female friends to our wives, to the women we work with, to female leaders in positions of authority around us. It's important to gather information about what we've experienced and what we've learned from those experiences. We do this work so we have the ability to transform what we've learned into new ways we want to behave.

For example, let's say your mother was controlling and demanding. So now, whenever your wife asks you to do something, even asking nicely, you hear it through the voice of your mother. Instead of responding to your wife with kindness, you use harsh language, frustration, or complete refusal in order to defend yourself from being told what to do. When you can go back and name where these feelings are coming from, you can then see that it isn't your wife you're responding to; it's your mother. But since you wouldn't address your mother in that way, out of fear or distorted loyalty, you hurt your wife in order to manage your pain.

It doesn't have to be this way. You can break the cycle by engaging (instead of avoiding) the pain you felt in the past and the sorrow you carry from it. You can learn to bring that to your wife so she can hold it with you, and you can learn healthier patterns of behavior together.

Dance of Desire and Devotion

The step we must take is from the safe embrace of our mother to the intoxicating embrace of our lover—the often frustrating, but necessary dance of desire and devotion where we temper what we want for who we want to become. Integrity within ourselves and security for those we claim to be devoted to is forged in these fires through intentional acts of self-control. These acts are not managed by discipline, but by devotion. Discipline can only get us so far, especially in the realm of sexuality.

This is why most men cycle through seasons of pornography. They have tried to place new boundaries in their lives and have sought to gain new tools through books and resources, as well as put in place new practices that arise through guilt and shame. But if the heart and value systems are not transformed, then the pornographic addiction or actions will return in time. For a man, behavior modification and moral superiority are not good enough motivators to change. He needs something to fight for, to contend against.

But more than just something to contend against, a man desires to have someone to fight alongside. Transformation is a difficult road and requires others on the journey with us or else we are in danger of isolating ourselves. One source of strength and support is meant to be found in a wife. This is the beauty of Genesis 1, the creation of Adam and Eve, made in the image of God. Eve was said to be a "helper," but the word is actually *'ēzer*, which is used twenty-one times in the Old Testament.[1] You can find it in the books of Exodus, Deuteronomy, Psalms, and Ezekiel, and each time, it is used in a military context. God even refers to Himself as Israel's *ʿēzer* in times of conflict, and you see images of spears, swords, victories, and deliverance connected to this word. This word refers to a warrior who fights with you in times of distress, who's not simply a sidekick. Your wife isn't simply there to help you accomplish what you want; she is someone you are to fight *alongside*, not *against*. She has resources you don't possess. To gain access to her intuition and wisdom, you will have to define what it is you're fighting for and learn how to fight differently.

Men have something to learn from the feminine, not just something to take from it. A woman's virginity, her purity, is a powerful teacher for men to temper their desires into willful sacrifice for the sake of honor and devotion, that we might learn from our lover even as we defend her. I love Condwiramurs's line that we find in our story: "If you do not seek to conquer me, I would like to come rest beside you." I chose to use the Wolfram version of her name, Condwiramurs, because the picture is an invitation to understand what it means to be a "lover" as a man, not just a sexual partner, or worse, an addict or someone uninterested in sex at all because it has lost its potency. And look at her language: *conquer* and *rest*. She is asking the question, "Can I trust you?"

This is the question of every woman to every man in the deepest parts of who she is. A woman would love to reveal the depths of herself emotionally, sexually, and spiritually to a man who would choose to protect her honor over selfishly attempting to steal from her. I don't care if a woman gave you consent; taking advantage of her is still your boyhood attempt to conquer, which gives you the false belief that you have claimed something of your manhood in the process. This is *not* the path of true biblical masculinity, and it *won't* be a great foundation for life-long devotion in marriage. Research shows that virgin couples who marry have the lowest divorce rates,[2] and married couples who have had fewer sexual partners in the past are consistently happier in their marriage.[3]

Sex Drive or Covenant Desire?

I understand that many people claim to have been wounded in the Church from what has become known as the "purity culture" or "purity movement," feeling shame and guilt about sex and sexuality both in experience and discussion. I'd like to offer a different perspective. My wife, after spending her young life in the world's version of sex and sexuality, received the beauty of the "purity message" as a breath of fresh air. It wasn't even an option to her in the world she came from. She witnessed peers in the Church attempting to live a lifestyle that was counterculture to anything else she had seen offered. Even though the movement's language may have been dysfunctional and the theology a bit distorted, for those who had been in the desert, it came as a glass of cold water.

I went through a "vow ceremony" myself in the purity movement and lived under its language in my junior high years. I ran from it in high school, but in the many opportunities I had to have sex, I knew I could choose something else. Several times I didn't choose otherwise, but I didn't believe I was condemned or wearing a scarlet letter because of it either. I recognized the weakness was in me, not in the message, and that I had areas of growth I needed to address. Every person has brokenness when it comes to sex and sexuality. Our experiences and exposure give us something to contend and wrestle with, but attempting to tame or even remove your God-given sexual desire as a man will never work. You must learn to temper it into something that helps you become who you were meant to be, instead of letting it hinder the life you were meant to lead.

151

The first step toward tempering your sexual desire as you encounter divine femininity is to realize that you do not have a "sex drive." This wording is not just a poor definition; it's psychologically, physiologically, and biologically untrue. For something in you to be defined as a drive, it must be something you will literally die from if left unsatisfied, like hunger or thirst or even sleep.

Let me put this more directly: You won't die from lack of orgasm. Although the lack may cause you discomfort or frustration, it's ultimately not life-threatening. Since that's the case, what if the desire in us that we're calling a sex drive isn't about sex at all, but is about sex as an expression of what our body is actually looking for—an intimate, committed connection with a woman we can defend and devote our life to?

I believe what we have isn't a sex drive, but is an unlocking of a covenant desire, which, when harnessed properly, can point us in the direction of a partner looking for the same thing. Sex in marriage isn't just for mutual pleasure or procreation; it's a sacrament. Like Communion reminds us of the covenant Christ made with us, sex in marriage is a reminder of the covenant you made with your spouse. Done regularly within the rhythms of family life, as well as across internal and external stressors, sex keeps us connected to one another in a way nothing else in marriage can. You can have deep conversations with friends, have fun, laugh, cry, and everything in between, but sex is reserved for just one person, your wife. Anything that comes between you and your wife, anything that makes sex difficult in your relationship, is a sign that something needs to be discussed and repaired, not ignored or swept under the rug. The desire in you is to be desired by the one your heart longs for. If there is no open dialogue about sex in your marriage, it will ultimately become a cause for fracture and frustration.

We have ignored our bodies for too long. Men push away and punish themselves for having needs and for attempting to do their caring in a way that will allow them to sustain longevity emotionally, physically, mentally, and spiritually. There is more to a man than simply pushing through and calling it sacrifice. It's only sacrificial if what you're giving has value to you. If you're sacrificing your body at work every day to make sure your family is provided for but you have no value for your body, then it's not a sacrifice; it's a waste. We must learn to listen to what our bodies are telling us.

The masculine road to connecting with your emotions doesn't begin with the heart; it begins with the body. For women, it's the opposite. They connect with their heart, and it moves to the body. It's because of men's overexposure to violence and sex that we have become too numb to our actual appetites. We can see this with food. We are so overindulged in junk food and drive-throughs that we don't know how to sustain lasting health. And if that's true of food, how much more of sex? Nearly every advertisement, every show, movie, and magazine, and every social media post is overtly sexual in nature, to the point that we cannot recognize what our actual appetite feels like anymore. We are ill-equipped to wrestle with the amount of sexual imagery and stimuli given to us on a regular basis. Maybe we could use a break from technology and all the images we take in daily. Maybe it would do our soul some good to sit still, in silence and solitude, for extended periods of time, and reset our connection to our body.

Do you know how unlikely it was to see a naked woman just one hundred years ago? Even just fifty years ago, when the first pornographic films were being released into culture, they were not readily available and in your pocket the way they are today. A man in those days would have had to go to great lengths to establish his health, occupation, and social status just to be considered for marriage, which was the only place most men would have ever encountered the naked female form. When a man did see a naked woman, it was a rarity, a curiosity.

In that same time period, the Church had a much larger religious influence within culture that created a stigma against pornography, which I would argue helped us more than the indulgence of instant gratification in every area of life that we experience today. Follow instant gratification up with legalized abortion and contraceptives so that no one has to be concerned with caring for an "unwanted" child, and you have a recipe for unrestrained sexual consumers instead of mature men with healthy and committed connections.

Before the age of widespread pornographic availability, men had to temper their appetites through work and sport. They married younger and stayed with their wife longer. They were built with something a little tougher than the men who are living in the post–sexual revolution culture we are steeped in today, combined with the lack of commitment to covenant rampant both in and out of the Church. I am not stating in any way that it was better back then or that they had it easier, I am simply attempting to show a progression of thought and the availability of sex as a culture. I don't have the space or the time to discuss the etymology of the word *passion* over several hundred years which went from exclusively meaning "the sufferings of Christ" to "intense sexual desire." We must learn how to engage in the struggle of managing our sexual desires regardless of culture, not just feed our sexual appetites with cheap images that domesticate our sexual imagination and sterilize our arousal experience.

▼ ▼ ▼

That morning, the two warriors faced off and charged at one another with pointed lances aimed to dismount each other. It wouldn't take long for both men to come off their horses. Young Parzival so wounded Kingrun that in his defeat, he began to plea for mercy.

Parzival immediately recalled the words of Gurnemanz: "In all of your courage and all of your fierceness, you must remember mercy." So the boy let Kingrun live and sent him to Camelot to work in the service of Cunneware, the woman of prophetic laughter. This would soon be the fate of all Parzival's vanquished knights. With their champion defeated and shamed, the army began to retreat, and the land was brought back to peace.

Parzival ran directly from the battlefield into the arms of Condwiramurs, who spoke, "Never will I marry anyone other than whom I have now embraced." As they embraced, two great ships from some foreign land sailed into the bay, loaded with food, wine, and treasures. Love itself brought provision to those in need. Love itself fed those who are starving, those lost in battle, those in fear. Because love was at the center, all were cared for, not just those in love, but those who stood under the covering of love's branches.

The two young lovers were married immediately; no need for long courtship rituals when the harp of love's song has been played. Their wedding chamber was full of nervous excitement. The young man stared at the body of his lover for what seemed like hours. *I dare not touch*, he thought to himself, so the first night was full of naive protocol and laughter at the innocence of their imagination. The second night was the same. Yet on the third night, they came together in the way that lovers have encountered one another since the beginning. They spent the whole of the night discovering their bodies for the first time. They both smiled and enjoyed each other's glow for days beyond that night together.

But this could not have happened if Parzival had known about the loss of his mother. Soon, he began to withdraw from his bride in the longing to know what had befallen his mother and what quests still lay ahead.

Many a man is searching for his mother when he enters into a union with his bride, if there is an unsettling in his soul that confuses him and causes him to search for that which isn't there. We don't know if it took months or a short few years for this to happen to Parzival, but we do know that the restlessness finally caught up with him.

Condwiramurs was distraught, but gave her support to him continuing his quest to find out what had become of his mother. Parzival left without knowing that his new bride was pregnant with twins.

▼ ▼ ▼

The mistakes of the father are repeated by the son. The Dark Knight left Herzeloyde when she was pregnant with Parzival, and now Parzival does the same to his wife.

This is the sad reality of generational trauma and pain that is undealt-with. The injury is passed on as a legacy to the next generation. We can call these curses if we need to, but I think if we were honest and didn't feel the need to spiritualize everything in order to give it value, the simple reality is that we will do to our sons what was done to us, because the cost to change our story is just too high. But this is not the end. Parzival has something beautiful to return to. As he rides away, his beloved does not fall to the floor dead, as his mother did in the forest.

There is hope for redemption when we meet a woman who knows who she is, who recognizes the strength she possesses, and who can see the glorious potential of the man she loves. When this part of the story comes to a close, we are not left hopeless; we are left with longing. Longing for our next encounter. Longing that breaks the cycles of rejection, abandonment, and avoidance. Believing that goodness can prevail and that God still has a plan.

THE WORK

Let's start by being honest. What about the feminine has hurt you? Don't start with your wife if you are married. Start with your mother, your first kiss, your first crush, an aunt, or maybe even just a female friend you had when you were little. What were your encounters with the feminine like growing up? When did you first notice the feminine in a way that was arousing or that made you think about your own sexuality? Just take a little time to explore the positive and negative impacts of these memories. What did you learn from them, and are you still responding to that today?

Also look at positive female role models who showed you what the caring, loving, nurturing side of the feminine can be like. Was there an encouraging teacher, friend, relative, or girl-friend who offered you a glimpse into divine femininity? Write about it. What specifically did you learn from those encounters and experiences? Are there things in those experiences you long for still, to this day? List them. Ask yourself if some of the expectations you are putting on the women in your life today might stem from some of these experiences.

Finally, I would like to encourage you to write a letter to your mother. You are not going to give this letter to her. This exercise is for you and should include these three things:

1. *Here is what I need to say to you about our relationship . . .*
   (Be honest and courageous.)

2. *Here is what I learned from you . . .*
   (Include one negative and one positive.)

3. *I forgive you for _____ . . .*
   (Then add what you are releasing her of.)

157

Take your time. Allow yourself to feel what happens in your body as you do these exercises. If it would be helpful to write a letter to another key woman in your life, I encourage you to do that as well. Allow yourself to grieve where needed, as well as to feel joy where it rises to the surface.

Path 9

Discovering True Strength by Embracing Failure

> A hero is someone who has given his or her life to something bigger than oneself.
>
> —Joseph Campbell, *The Power of Myth*

Failure is not supposed to be fatal, but in a culture of perfectly curated, cropped, and filtered images available for daily consumption 24/7, it's hard to remember that. When everyone else's lives look so put together and they seem to get everything you've ever wanted with such ease, it can be difficult to combat the onslaught mentally and emotionally. Yet we have to remember that the filtered images are not real. Life is full of devastating disappointments and brutal letdowns for all of us, brought on by poor judgment and immature decisions we've made. Many of these have to do with the fact that we don't know what we're doing and we feel alone in our journey. How can you be expected to love and support your wife well and invest in your children in ways that will help them grow into healthy adults, let alone wrestle with your sexuality and spirituality in ways that grow you into maturity, when no one took the time to teach you how to do it?

I'm not attempting to let men off the hook for childish behavior or flawed attempts at self-management. I just want you to understand where these come from so you can begin the process of transformation. If you believe failure is fatal and the mistakes of your past (even your recent past) define you, then you will allow shame and guilt to tell your story instead of grace and mercy. You limit your potential for growth if you have already predetermined that you will fail and that any attempt to change is fruitless.

This is why most men don't engage in the work of transformation. They already feel the weight of the world on their shoulders, and they don't know what to do with it. They want to love their wife, but she isn't able to receive it. They want to engage spiritually, but don't feel smart. They radically love their children, but feel as though they have nothing to offer them. Let me make this clear after years of working with men and couples: *you are not alone.*

▼ ▼ ▼

As Parzival's horse surged out across the most desolate landscapes, thoughts of his mother clouded images of Condwiramurs—a mix of sadness and beauty, desire and desperation. He found no sanctuary in his soul where the pain of his wondering could be stored, so he continued fighting his way through bogs and fields where animals were found competing over scraps, and through villages where men were empty of strength and women were lonely of heart. The land itself seemed tormented in some deep way.

Toward dusk one evening, Parzival came upon a lake surrounded by a black forest. At the center of the lake, he saw a man fishing on a small boat. He recognized that this man wasn't clothed like a man of the country or village. In fact, what he noticed first was the large peacock feather from the man's hat waving in the breeze, as if to welcome him. Yet he could tell even from this great distance that the man carried a sadness that in some way reminded him of himself. So he called out to the man, "Do you know of where I might find shelter for the evening?"

The sadness Parzival assumed from the man's posture was confirmed in his voice as he responded, "There is no place within thirty miles in any direction, but you are welcome in my home." The man added, "Head to the cliff's end, and then make a right, and you will find yourself before the moat of my castle. But I warn you not to veer to the left or right; do not get distracted. These woods are dangerous, and you would be wise to stay on course until your arrival."

Parzival did not hesitate. He thanked the angler and turned his horse in the direction given. As he came around the bend, his eyes were overwhelmed by the sight of magnificent castle walls so high it was said you had to have the wings of an angel to scale them. This was the imposing Grail Castle.

Our young hero stood in awe, but was completely unaware of what he was approaching. The drawbridge was lowered, as if he had been expected. The large wooden beams clad in iron spanned the dark waters of the moat to grant him access to the interior of this holy structure. Yet just as he crossed it, the drawbridge snapped shut tightly and nipped the back hooves of his horse, causing it to buck and squeal, and almost knocking Parzival completely off in front of the many attendants now surrounding him.

▼ ▼ ▼

It is like this for all who enter the Grail Castle. Many a youth has been unhorsed attempting to make the transition from the ordinary world to the beauty and mystery of the symbolic world of that place. Many things we think will carry us into its depths are usually worthless in a space like this. We are entering holy ground. Our shoes must come off, and we must hold close our humility, lest we be humbled.

The Spanish poet Antonio Machado once said, "Mankind owns four things that are no good at sea: rudder, anchor, oars, and the fear of going down."[1] We cannot attempt to steer, stop, control, or respond in fear; we simply must keep moving forward. This is the only course of action available to us. You are not in competition with anyone but the you from twenty-four hours ago. Did you move a little farther down the path today? Just one tiny step a day can make all the difference. Even if the step feels backward, if you will learn from it in humility, you can make it a step forward. What will you do with the opportunities you've been given? As you transition into maturity, don't let the experiences of the past unhorse you as you move into the place of mystery and tension, wrestling with where you are today and the possibility of where you could be in ten years.

▼ ▼ ▼

Four young attendants took Parzival's horse and brought the young man in to bathe him and give him fresh clothing. Everything was taken to be cleaned except the tunic his mother had given him. Then he was led to the center of the castle to sit before the master, the Great Grail King, the Fisher King, his given name Anfortas, or "infirmity."

The king was opposite the entrance, lying on a couch next to a great fire. The room was filled with large, beautiful chandeliers the likes of which Parzival had never seen. He was led over to sit with the king and immediately bore witness to the king's pain.

The Grail King quickly apologized for being unable to rise and greet Parzival properly, due to his wound. But even amid all the pain the king attempted to conceal, Parzival would say that Anfortas was still the most beautiful man he had ever seen. Seated next to the fire, clad in black and gray, the king had a head full of white hair. Atop it sat a fur beret that held at its center the purest ruby any eyes had ever taken in. The Grail King looked both ancient and youthful at the same time, and it was hard for Parzival not to stare at him to examine him.

Then, quite gently, a procession began, like the tender beginning of a musical score that invites you to pay attention because something is coming you won't want to miss. The imagery felt intentional, and not one detail was out of place. First, a young man entered the room with a lance that seemed to weep blood. Some will tell you it was the lance that had pierced the side of Christ. This boy was moaning quietly, tears running down his face, and the entire room grieved as he paraded the lance around it.

Then he departed as two beautiful young maidens entered. Each wore flower garlands in her long, thick, golden hair, and each carried an ornate, exquisite candelabra, with candles flickering their delicate light upon the room. Behind these two maidens other women proceeded, with deep golden curls down to their waists, scarlet robes, and golden dresses highlighted in emerald. These carried in cutlery and more candelabras. Even more immaculate maidens followed. Eighteen in all had gathered, wearing colors of earthy brown and scarlet red, with waistbands and sashes of emerald and gold. They gathered and eagerly waited for what was about to come.

Then the Grail King's sister, Repanse, entered the room, and everyone thought the sun had risen in the middle of the night. She carried a stone they called the Grail, and Parzival found it hard even to look at it, despite wanting to stare.

The Grail was brought before the great crippled king and set down. Magic filled the air. There was a sense that anything was possible in that atmosphere, that death and life were one and the same, that the natural and supernatural divide was blurred, and that you could reach out and touch heaven itself. In the presence of the Grail, the world itself could find peace, all soil could produce fruit, the seas and the air would clear, and nature and humanity would reconcile themselves to one another.

Then immediately, as if from nowhere and everywhere at the same time, one hundred tables were brought in with fresh linen. Gold platters filled with food and drink were set out around the room. The king, in pain, washed his hands. Parzival did the same.

Although they were eating together, it appeared that every time Parzival lifted his head the whole room looked to him, waiting in suspense for whatever he might say. But he dared not say a word. He remembered the strict words of Gurnemanz: "Never ask too many questions. Be silent in the presence of greatness and glory."

Right then, without that advice, all could have been made right. The king would have been healed, and the land restored. But no words left Parzival's mouth.

▼ ▼ ▼

Many a young man has been here before, stumbling into a place of great depth and unimaginable beauty. Maybe it's when he first awakens to the enchanting form of the feminine. Maybe it's when he encounters God in an unexpected way or wanders into a holy place. Maybe it happens for him when he is exposed to the immensity of nature, and it reminds him how small he really is in the context of all time and space.

But we're unprepared to give language to it, to understand what is truly at hand and what it may cost, if we aren't able to ask the necessary questions and discover what these moments are really offering us. The cost is too great, the imagery too grand, and a man's pain too deep. We don't want to mess it up or blow it, so instead we do nothing, missing dozens, or hundreds, of transforming moments simply because we weren't able to open our mouths and humble our hearts.

This isn't a guilt trip, as much as an invitation. Maybe we need to stop being silent and feeling stupid, and have the courage to engage with each opportunity as it presents itself to us. I understand the difficulty, the harsh words that echo in our heads, the past moments where we felt that we asked the wrong question or others laughed at us. I can truly see how much a man has to overcome in order to engage with situations and circumstances that reveal how little he thinks he knows about himself and the world around him. But this is not a reason to retreat; it's a divine opportunity to heal, for us and for those we encounter along the way.

▼ ▼ ▼

In one last attempt to move his guest to speak, the Grail King offers young Parzival a gift: "Please, young sir, take this sword that has been by my side in many a battle, until God saw fit to wound me past all measure. I have used it to strike down foe and warrior. Its forging is not of human origin, and it would be an honor for you to bear it now and use it as you see fit. I hope it makes up for any lack in our service to you here today."

Parzival wanted to speak, to say something—anything. But his loyalty to Gurnemanz and his fear of speaking out of turn stopped him. He nodded his head as he gracefully accepted the sword.

The king slumped back in pain, realizing he could do no more to prompt the boy. At this, the meal came to an abrupt end. Every maiden and squire left the room, briefly glimpsing the beautiful old man on their way out. Finally, the king stated simply that Parzival must be tired and that he should make his way to his chambers.

Maidens met Parzival at his room and helped him change for his evening rest. Pages bearing candlesticks with dancing flames laid out fruit and wine that some claim were from Eden itself. They set the food before him on the purest white linen cloth, and he partook of just enough to honor their service. But he longed to retreat under his covers, a great warrior hiding under sheets of linen and silk.

They left him in peace, but his sleep carried nothing of peace with it. Plagued with dreams of his mother, teeth gnashing and sweat breaking, he prayed for the dawn. And when it came, the entire castle was silent, as if it had been abandoned in the night. Parzival's restlessness gave way to wonder as dawn began to break and no maidens or pages came to assist him. His weariness from lack of sleep gave way to another restless moment of slumber before he awoke again and realized that it was nearly midday and the castle sounded empty and abandoned.

Seeing his two swords near the bedside, Parzival got out of bed and grabbed them both, including the one given to him by the Grail King. He dressed himself quickly and wandered curiously down the chilly halls of the now abandoned castle. When he wandered into the courtyard, he was relieved to find his horse waiting for him, as if prepared for him before all had left this lonely, untamable place. He mounted his steed and slowly trotted across the drawbridge.

Suddenly, a hidden vassal drew the bridge up so quickly that it clipped the horse's hooves again, as on the way in. The horse almost threw its rider from his saddle, and then a haunting voice cried out to him, "You are a goose! If you had but opened your mouth, you could have had it and so much more. All that was required was that you ask the right question."

Our young hero cried out for explanation, but nothing was offered him. Silence was the only reply. What was he supposed to know? Was there something he had missed? Still, silence. Whatever nobility and pride Parzival had felt before going into that castle now fell from his body into the mud as he galloped away into the next battle, the Grail Castle slowing fading from view.

▼ ▼ ▼

Parzival's problem wasn't just the terrible advice from a broken mentor. It was also the memory of his mother, the twisted advice she had given him, and most importantly, the symbolism of the homespun sackcloth still found underneath his armor. No man can relate to the Grail in any permanent way if he's still being covered by his mother underneath all his masculine exploits and victories. Deep spirituality for a man requires that he actually "leaves and cleaves." He must lead his family and love his wife without leaning back into the arms and the bosom of his waiting mother.

In all of this we have a picture of what the heart of a true mother should represent—safety, security, comfort, and gentleness. Yet a devoted mother like Parzival's can long for a man to conform, play it safe, and not get hurt. This is not because the mother doesn't want her son to grow; it's because above anything else, she would rather know he is safe. Rumi, the great thirteenth-century Sufi mystic, wrote about this in his poem called "The Core of Masculinity": "Your old grandmother says, 'Maybe you shouldn't go to school. You look a little pale.' Run when you hear that."[2] Rumi finishes by exalting the sternness of a good father, who tempers his son with discipline into who he was meant to be, to bear the weight and responsibility of true masculinity.

You may have been born a male, but masculinity requires more from us. You must be trained; you must be walked into it. Initiation for a boy is an invitation, but it's not an option. The heart of a mother wants to make sure you are okay; the heart of a father wants to make you dangerous. Notice I did not say *reckless*. That's different. Meekness within a man is formed when he is able to recognize and own his potential for destruction and harness it for the protection and provision of others.

Avoid Getting too Comfortable

We must avoid our attempts to be too comfortable. They keep the most powerful parts of us domesticated in an attempt to be welcomed into predominately feminine environments, or to become more feminine in order to make others more comfortable with us. For men, this reveals itself in the form of daily tension as they attempt to be aware of their emotions without being led by them. Parzival wanted to speak; he knew he should speak. The emotion of his moment with the Grail King was captivating, but because he hadn't been taught how to translate it into appropriate language, he defaulted into what he had seen from other men and what his mentor had offered him: "Say nothing when it gets overwhelming or when you find yourself in the presence of greatness."

So it is today with so many men. Silence grips their lips because they haven't been taught to dialogue with experiences like this. We need to find our courage and define our language.

The remainder of our story, all the adventures and all the quests, will be about Parzival moving toward the removal of those homespun rags made by his mother. He doesn't stop loving or honoring her, but so long as a man is encased in his mother complex, he cannot appreciate the Grail or ask the right question.

In fact, many men find the whole experience of the Grail Castle (in some tales called the Wild Mountain) and their failure there so painful, so incomprehensible, that they immediately repress it and say they don't remember it at all. Part of the disappearing of the castle itself is that most men never want to see it or deal with it ever again. They will settle for anything if you indirectly call it a grail: sex, drugs, money, fame, success. It's all just a form of escapism.

Even religion itself, or nationalism, can give a man the ecstasy of questing for the Grail, without the cost of looking at his own failure. But this experience of failure, of frustration with self and circumstances, is a necessary part of the process. You simply cannot move forward in who you are if you aren't willing to look at what you still lack.

▼ ▼ ▼

Parzival wanted nothing to do with the Grail Castle, the Grail King, the whole experience. He simply wanted to find the next battle and charged out into the forest with no direction in mind. He determined to earn the sword he was given at Grail Castle; it was the least he could offer this experience.

Along his way, however, his grief caught up with him and he began to weep. Then through his lonely tears, he heard the tears of another. He followed the sound, drying his eyes as he went. Slowly, he came upon a woman holding in her arms a knight embalmed and wrapped for burial. Parzival had unknowingly stumbled upon his cousin Sigune once again, still stricken with grief and now clinging to the body of her dead husband. But his weary eyes, swollen from tears, didn't recognize her, with her face covered by the hood of a mourning widow. As he approached, he wanted to avoid this situation altogether, but the grief of another somehow drew him, and he asked if there was anything he could do.

Sigune recognized Parzival immediately and questioned him: "Where did you stay last night? Where are you coming from?" She knew there was nothing for many miles around except the opulence of a castle rarely seen by human eyes. She described Grail Castle, and Parzival said it was, in fact, where he had stayed.

At this, Sigune's eyes brightened and her mood completely changed. "You saw the Grail! You must have asked the question! You can't find that castle simply by looking for it. It's a mystery how one encounters it, but you, Parzival, have been there! I recognize that sword you wear at your side. It belonged to the Fisher King. How I have wished he could be released from his suffering. What was it like there? What was the question you asked?"

Afraid and humiliated, Parzival told the truth: "I said nothing."

Sigune's mood altered again. "I hate that I have seen you and heard this news!" she exclaimed. "My grief is now multiplied! All this suffering, all these people, all this land could have been restored if you would have simply opened your mouth. You have betrayed us all. Your heart is cold and your soul stained, that you could not bear witness to the Grail King's pain. You have soiled your knighthood, and your reputation will go before you and defile any attempts at worthiness in any realm."

"Be kind!" Parzival said. "I did not know! I will return to the castle and make it right!"

Sigune replied, "That's a fool's errand. Grail Castle isn't found by those who look for it. You threw away the one chance you had in this life. Get away from me! I cannot bear to look at you any longer."

With that, Parzival turned his face from her and wandered away. As she returned to her grief, Parzival returned to his deep humiliation and lonely sorrow. Deeper into the strange forest he went. The day grew warmer, and his head grew heavy. He took off his helmet so the breeze would touch his damp face and bring a little bit of ease to his wanderings.

Further ahead, he noticed yet another woman riding on a wretched nag, wearing tattered and torn garments and looking weary beyond telling. As she approached him on his path, she urged Parzival to run, to choose another direction quickly. He immediately recognized Jeschute, the woman from the pavilion on his first day leaving his mother's home. She told him that Orilus, her beloved, was just up ahead and was still angry over what Parzival had done, claiming revenge upon him.

Parzival put his helmet back on and turned around just in time to see his opponent across the quiet meadow. The two men lowered the visors upon their helmets, grabbed their lances, and charged across the fiery green blades of grass glowing in the afternoon sun.

Parzival easily unmounted Orilus and pounced on him, drawing his sword and demanding that he yield. Orilus was undone by such a defeat. He had never lost in battle before and was taken aback by the ferocity and mercy of this man. He knew Parzival must have goodness in him, and there must be a misunderstanding between them. Parzival apologized for his earlier indiscretions and was able to return the ring he had taken from Jeschute, thus proving his innocence with her.

Orilus moved toward Jeschute and said he was sorry for not believing her or trusting her. She forgave him, and they embraced fully and tenderly as he gently kissed her upon the brow. But the defeated knight must suffer the consequences of his loss, and Parzival told him he must travel to King Arthur's court and go into the service of Lady Cunneware, as had so many other knights Parzival had defeated. This was even worse than defeat for Orilus, who lowered his head and explained that Cunneware is his sister. Now, due to his hot temper and lack of trust in his beloved, he must place himself in service to her.

Parzival bid them farewell and wandered into the woods as Orilus and Jeschute set off to find Arthur and his court. It just so happens that Arthur and his knights were not too far away, searching for the Red Knight. When the two found Lady Cunneware with them, she recognized her brother and the humility he had just faced. She acknowledged the remorse he felt and released him from his vow of service. She truly believed there was goodness within him.

Arthur and his Knights of the Round Table desired the Red Knight to join them. It was hard to deny his deeds and his value for the court when he had been sending so many worthy knights back to serve after bringing them to defeat by his sword and spear. Little did they know Parzival, the one they sought, was just a few miles away. He was lost, alone, and cold, for an early snow had blown in and a light remnant was upon the ground.

One of King Arthur's prized falcons had been lost from his camp. Being overfed, it had left in search of hunting grounds and desired to spread its wings. What it found instead was Parzival. It came to rest near him as he set up his camp to lie down for the night. As the sun crept into the sky in the early hours of dawn, a large flock of geese settled in the open meadow near them. As rider and falcon rose, the geese took off in unison, making a large, unearthly noise. The falcon followed as the geese climbed into the sky. One goose was caught in the talons of Arthur's mighty falcon, just enough to cause three drops of blood to fall in front of Parzival, who had just mounted his horse in full battle gear in an attempt to stay warm. As those three drops fell, Parzival became enraptured in a lover's trance. The snow reminded him of the fair skin of his beloved, and the red of her lips and rosy cheeks. He could not think of or see anything else, his eyes transfixed upon the ground. He missed Condwiramurs, longed for her, desired to find her and be with her.

At that moment one of Arthur's attendants, searching for the falcon, came upon the Red Knight seemingly girded for battle, lance erect in the air, a sign of challenge. The young attendant didn't recognize him and ran back to the camp to tell Arthur of the shameless intruder. Kai spoke up first and asked to challenge this knight. Arthur agreed, and Kai set out. He saw Parzival from across the meadow, lowered his lance, and charged with all his might.

Parzival did not move, still in a trance, lost in deep longing for Condwiramurs. His response to the onslaught was purely a reflex, killing the horse and launching Kai into a fallen tree. Upon impact, Kai broke his leg and arm, fulfilling a promise Parzival spoke when Kai mistreated Lady Cunneware earlier in our story.

Kai was completely enraged and embarrassed by what had befallen him. His young squire took him back to Arthur's camp, where he explained in great detail what took place. Gawain, who just recently had arrived, mocked Kai and jested at what he experienced. Then Gawain asked if he could go meet the knight who had just done such a thing.

Arthur again agreed to the proposal. Gawain took no lance, no sword, no armor, but went out to approach the knight. Immediately, he recognized it was Parzival, the Red Knight, the one they'd been searching for. He saw that Parzival was in a lover's trance. Having been there many times himself, he was aware that Parzival was lost in heart and must be woken up. Gawain took off his green cloak and laid it over the three drops of blood.

Parzival looked up in fear and drew his sword on the knight before him. Gawain explained the situation and how he had found him, and offered to lead him to Arthur, where the court awaited him in camp. This brought a sense of peace to the young man's heart, and he followed willingly.

As they arrived, Arthur threw his arms around the Red Knight and welcomed him. A celebration began, the likes of which Parzival hadn't experienced in what felt like ages. They feasted, they laughed, they drank, they told old stories. Parzival told all he had experienced, all but the Grail Castle, which for that brief moment he was able to forget and ignore.

Lady Cunneware joined the celebration and brought Parzival new clothing and fine coverings for his generosity and kindness toward her. With so many knights in her service, she had need of nothing and was honored among women.

Parzival's ego was fulfilled, and his heart lost its grieving and indulged in being celebrated. Each knight told of his respect for the Red Knight, and of his excitement at having him in their company. This felt as if things were changing. This would be a fresh start, a new beginning for Parzival. He could move on from what he had missed. There was no need to bring up the past or return to wandering aimlessly in the wilderness any longer.

But this celebration was short-lived. Out of the forest something vile came riding in on a great steed black as night, with a mane blowing in a wind not there, and steam and smoking fire burning from its two angry nostrils. The creature mounted on its back was able with a dark chuckle to remove all merriment from this gathering. Her red eyes flamed as she scanned the room. From the hole in her face that served for a mouth, two giant yellow boar tusks jutted out, glimmering in the light of the moon and the fiery torches surrounding the table. Her nose was like that of a dog, and she had the ears of a bear. Her nails were like that of a lion, with dirt and filth under each one. The skin they could see was pale, almost green, with a light covering of tough fur. Her hair was an unwashed dark brown, either from the color or the years. She wore a London hat laden with peacock feathers, and a hooded cloak of silk cut in the French style. She spoke three languages: Latin, Arabic, and French. She was skilled in the movement of the stars, she was a virgin, and she was a truth teller. She was the great Grail defender. Her name was Cundry. She terrified the men of Arthur's court, and most especially Parzival.

Cundry stood in their midst with her scathing gaze directed toward King Arthur. She spoke in French as she addressed him with such disgust that the skin crawled on all who had to witness this unearthly sight: "You have disgraced your father's table, and you undo his good name. The honor that you once knew is mixed with gall and is nullified by whom you will allow at your table. You praise the knight in red, Parzival, but it's nothing but a costume, a forgery."

She then whipped around to face Parzival and spoke: "You are to blame for my arrival, for my unwelcome greeting. You sat in the presence of the Fisher King, the Grail before you. You watched him grieve and said nothing. You did not ask the question, and therefore oppressed us all. You are a faithless, inconsiderate fool. You lack anything of manhood within you, and all men of great worth will reject you. You are unworthy of your name, and your failure shall be your only fame. I will continue, and you will heed my words. Did you know you had a brother? Feirefiz of Angevin, born of another country's noble queen, although you share a father. You are both sons of Gahmuret, a courageous warrior and gracious king. Your brother is a wonderous man, a sight to behold, with skin mixed black and white, like that of a magpie. But your father's honor you have undone in just one ignorant action."

With that, she scolded Gawain and Arthur again. Then she left as quickly as she had entered, leaving many in tears and shocked by the accusations she had laid before them.

Parzival began his justification by blaming Gurnemanz and the advice he took from him. But it didn't matter; the damage was done. The truth had been revealed that he had not asked the question and had left the Grail King and the land in pain.

Parzival gathered his things and mounted his horse to head back into the wilderness. As he was about to leave, Gawain offered a blessing on him: "I know that wherever you go, you will face great hardship and much trouble, but I ask that God would grant you success in this journey."

As Parzival tured away, head hung low, he simply asked, "What is God?"

▼ ▼ ▼

Men need someone who will unapologetically call them on their secrets and hold them accountable to their actions. The female form of this, represented in our story by Cundry, can be dangerous to men who are struggling with insecurity and lack of identity. When a female points out what we already know but have chosen to ignore, we become resistant and resentful toward the woman who dares point to the place in our life where we still need healing and growth. Yet this is an opportunity for vulnerability, to own the truth of who we are in front of others. I understand that having your weakness pointed out through failure may feel like criticism (and maybe sometimes it is), but can it really be criticism if what the woman says of us is true?

Our wives access this energy and position of Cundry the crone consistently, and we reject them when they should be celebrated. They are attempting to call us into our fullness by exposing places where we lack, and they may be the only ones who see it. I'm not saying their delivery is always the best, or their language or timing could never be better. But your wife must speak, because she is more concerned with you becoming who you were meant to be than she is about how you feel about it.

This is a characteristic of Cundry the crone, the dangerous old woman whom every woman should be attempting to grow into as she ages—in the sense of being a woman in touch with her intuition, who can access the courage to say things to us no one else would say. In myth, you get either the crone or the witch. The witch is an evil being, purely malevolent in intent. But the crone is a dangerous old woman who may appear to be a witch, but who is actually guiding us into our destiny with unconventional tactics. The conviction and direction such a woman's words bring can cut us to our core, but they are ultimately the shaking we need to move forward in our story. It may not feel good to discover our weakness through failure in this way, but it is good for us on our journey toward biblical masculinity. It reminds us of the work that is still needed and calls us to something more than we could ever have imagined possible.

THE WORK

If you want to discover true strength beyond your failures and beyond the experiences you feel have betrayed you, then here's the challenge: If it's safe, and you feel as if you and your wife are in a place to do this without damaging each other or your relationship, then let her know that you would like to talk sometime about areas you could grow in. Ask when a good time would be for her. Don't ask her in passing or when she's busy. Give her time to respond.

Then, when she's ready, grab a piece of paper and a pen and ask your wife to give you three specific areas or actions that you need to grow in, areas that would make her feel loved and would help you become who you were meant to be. Ask for clarification where needed. Don't justify, don't argue. Just write the three areas down and thank her for her insights.

If you are single or are not in a place with your wife where you can do this positively, consider speaking with a man in your life who knows you well enough and is brave enough to talk with you about areas you need to strengthen. Don't look for a person who is too safe and who won't ask the hard questions. Find someone you are a little scared to talk with—a pastor, a teacher, a grandfather, another leader, someone whom it will cost you to converse with.

Once you've had the enlightening discussion, from there you can explore three questions within each area or action you were offered:

1. *What do I feel when I hear this?*
    Write it out. Really engage with it, even noticing where you feel it in your body. (You can refer to appendix IV's "Body Sensations List" if you need help identifying such feelings.)

176

2. *Where do I see this in my life?*

   What are some key places in your life where you can really see this area and its effects?

3. *What's one small step I can take today to grow in this area?*

   Don't overthink this. Make it small and make it tangible. Our goal here is practice. Receive something that's hard to hear, and grow from it.

Again, make sure to journal the entire process. Then come back to it in a few weeks or months and chart your growth.

Path 10

Engaging in the Redemptive Work of Grief

> Furthermore, we have not even to risk the adventure alone;
> for the heroes of all time have gone before us; the labyrinth
> is thoroughly known; we have only to follow the thread of
> the hero-path.
>
> —Joseph Campbell, *The Hero with a Thousand Faces*

I don't know who said it. Maybe it was me, or maybe I read it somewhere. This is probably a distilled version of both, but I believe that we as a culture are "grief illiterate," choosing to live in a state of amnesia and anesthesia, with unexpressed sorrow often showing up as anxiety, depression, and addiction. The answer to this is that we desperately need God. Not just the convenient, institutionalized version of religion regulated to lethargic church meetings, but the awe-inspiring, majestic, holy God of the Bible.

We don't need Him just for evangelical exploits; we need Him to wake us up—wake us up to eternity, to His story, to our story, to our humbling place in history, and to the beauty of our brokenness. We need to be humbled. The humiliation we saw our hero face in the previous chapter will bear the fruit necessary for him to encounter the reality of God again, even with his departing phrase, "What is God?"

The crone Cundry necessarily humiliates Parzival in front of all his peers, so that he might be humbled in all the right areas to begin the process of transformation. That process always begins with a return to God. I once heard someone say that he would regularly pray to God, *Judge me now so you don't have to judge me later.* This is what Parzival just experienced, and it's what we need to experience in our lives, remembering that while we were still sinners Christ died for us, not after we had it all together and were able to articulate the right theology accurately. We need to experience this depth of love if we are ever going to see redemption in our own story and share that redemption with others.

We must make agreement with our great defeats and hear the echoes of their deafening sorrow in our daily life. Doing so proves the nature of reality itself, that "glory to glory" isn't some perfect upward trend, with life getting better and better with each passing year. Rather, it's a collection of thousands of ups and downs that remind us of our deep need for connection with God and connection with others. God told us to have courage because He knew we would experience moments of fear. He encouraged us to have faith because He knew we would walk through seasons of doubt. This is life—mountains and valleys, highs and lows, making up one complex and powerful story.

Mercy More Powerful than Shame

What do we do when everywhere we go appears to be a valley? When all seems lost, and simply making it through the day feels like an impossible task due to the unbearable weight of our shame and failures? We learn the movement of mercy and the sound of its enrapturing melody. Learning to accept mercy for ourselves is much harder than offering it to others, because we know what we've done, the opportunities we've had, and how we've crumbled under pressure when presented with the right choices. We instead let shame tell our story and let our failures have authority over who we become and how we live.

But these are not our only options. Mercy and grace have something to say to us as we offer ourselves kindness and begin to do the work of grief. Our ego is the enemy of the greatness inside us; it locks the truest form of who we are behind the lies that we are not enough and what we've done is so devasting that restoration is not an option. The reason we don't know how to love our enemies is because we haven't learned to love ourselves. When we cannot accept the wrong we've done, we'll never be able to accept the wrong others have done, even our children or our spouse. Learning to love ourselves doesn't begin with thinking happy thoughts or having some delusional positive attitude that fades every time no one is looking. It begins with truth, followed by grief.

This is why a Cundry figure in our life is so valuable, why our wife calling us on all our crap, and having real friends who point out what we still need to work on, is something we cannot live without. It shakes us from our apathy, from our hiddenness, and exposes us so we have to deal with reality and come out of hiding.

But this is not easy work. You can accept it or defend against it, but it doesn't make it less true. The only way to engage with reality is truth, and the greatest assistance to truth is mercy. If we are able to experience mercy, then maybe we will be able to tell the truth and live with the lights on. But someone or something has to stop us on our journey of self-pity and victimization and point us back to God, if we're ever going to encounter a mercy more powerful than our shame.

▼ ▼ ▼

In the years that followed, Parzival had many adventures and went on many quests. The time and the number we cannot count. He battled to forget, but at times his eyes glazed over in an unearthly daydream about Grail Castle, the Grail King, and the Grail. It haunted him, and he wandered lost and alone through the great mud of his own failures.

Some storytellers would say that in this season he was pursuing Cundry even more than the castle, that there was something of under-standing he required of her so he would know what he might do next. He would catch glimpses of her on a trail here and there, but she eluded him. So he quested on. No conquest, no proud victory seemed to quiet the ache in his heart, and the Wild Mountain itself left a void that nothing was able to fill. It was as if God Himself had fallen silent.

But this road would not be in vain. Parzival stumbled once more upon his cousin Sigune as he pursued a fresh trail left by Cundry. Sigune apologized for her frustration and bitterness the last time they had met, and she told him that Cundry had recently been there. It was the crone who brought provision to Sigune from the castle Parzival's heart was seeking.

Sigune then blessed Parzival and prayed that God's hand would guide him through his sorrow, to find joy again and rest for his heart. He thanked her and wandered on, frustrated that the castle and Grail had eluded him so. His path led him, as it had so many times before, into yet another battle. A knight stood in his way without a helmet upon his head and demanded that Parzival leave these grounds. He warned him of what would then ensue, donned his helmet, and began to charge.

The knight was thrown into a gully by Parzival's mighty blow. He wasn't killed, but he was left in pain, attempting to drag himself from his position. Although this duel didn't take his life, it did take the life of

Parzival's steed. Seeing the horse of his defeated foe caught in the wild brush, he mounted that knight's steed and rode further into the forest.

As Parzival slumped along the path, in misery and loneliness of heart, he stumbled upon a small group of pilgrims. With them was a grizzled old knight whose beard was the grayest he had ever seen, accented by his gray, coarse clothing that seemed harsh and uninviting. The knight was walking with his wife and their two daughters and carried no signs of wealth or position.

Parzival greeted the family somberly, and the aging knight gently asked him why he was armed on such a day. Parzival clearly didn't understand the question, and the gray knight told him it was Good Friday, adding, "This is a holy day, a day of great joy and great sorrow, the day the world joins together to recognize the great kindness and love shown in the sacrifice of the God-Man, Jesus. If you have been baptized, then I urge you to join us. Remove your armor, and come sit with us awhile."

One of his daughters spoke up: "Father, let us lead him to the fire. The weather has turned, and we are all freezing."

The old knight agreed and went on to speak of a holy man they would visit with during this time. He urged that Parzival should join them by the fire, warm himself, and find the holy advice he appeared to be in search of.

Parzival wanted nothing to do with God. He felt the pilgrims' God had abandoned him and left him on this trail. He wanted to ride away in anger and reject that anyone should follow a God who had denied him the help he so desperately sought. But something drew him. Was it his mother's teachings? The longing to believe that there was still hope for him? He rode with the pilgrims for a short time, still deciding what to do. Then resolved, he spurred the horse forward to a hermit's cell, a small cave, the residence of the pious Trevrizent.

Parzival tethered his horse in a shaded portion of the cliff, near a snowy waterfall, and immediately recognized that the occupant of this humble cave was no simple monk. He was a man and warrior-poet who had experienced both love and loss, the ecstasy of intimate connection and the devastating throes of rejection. The old storytellers say Trevrizent was a celibate man and was fasting when Parzival met him, having given up food for a hunger greater than that of the world. His eyes were resolute, his body strengthened from the daily life of one who worked the earth to reap its rewards.

The two men gathered simple food for the horse, and then Trevrizent led Parzival to a bed where he could yield his armor. He relinquished all but his mother's tunic as he borrowed a humble cloak from the hermit. As he stood near the fire, it warmed him down to his bones. The champion and the hermit settled in to do the work necessary for the continuation of Parzival's journey.

▼ ▼ ▼

There must be more for us as men than engaging in the next battle or conquest in a vain attempt to avoid and deflect the guilt and shame we feel. Even our serving, our religious work, and all our sacrifices become another opportunity to prove our "goodness" through platitudes and performance, which ultimately leaves us in the same mess that got us there in the first place. We give the outward appearance of devotion, with nothing sustainable on the inside. We move to greater acts of devotion, while the devastating pain of our true self is covered by an imposter who gets us what we need to make it through another day.

We give ourselves to our "calling" as a cover, which is why so many broken people find their way into Church leadership. We want to cover up our past and current transgressions with duty and service to God, yet we wonder why we still don't feel or see any real change in our lives. And we wonder why those we love are frustrated with our empty words and fruitless lifestyle. We want to participate in God's redemptive work in the world, but we've lost ourselves along the way, looking over our shoulder for Grail Castle and the king we let down.

Needed: A Man with Experience

In this space or season of our life, we need a man with some experience. We need a prophet and priest to walk us through the gauntlet of failures that mark and mar our true identity. Only a man whose life has been set apart from the cultural ladders others are attempting to climb will do. When we meet Trevrizent in our story, he is celibate, fasting, and living in a cave outside the village, near the edge of the forest, between civility and the wild. He is an image of John the Baptist, calling the religious and irreligious to a higher standard. He seems mythological in nature and otherworldly in his appearance. All of this gives him the ability to strike deep at the heart of what's actually happening, because in him there is no compromise.

Where are such men today? The wise elders who cannot be swayed by finance or fame, who keep their hearts on fire so young men can warm themselves near the flame? These wise men have authority to speak and hold space for us because they don't need us to like them in order to feel successful about their lives. We need men like this, and when we cannot find the men we need, we must become them. If you're looking around and desire this type of influence in your life, but you've never come across such a creature, then it's an invitation to become such a one. The road will be difficult and filled with danger, but it will be worth it for all those you encounter over the course of your life. It's all a divine setup to redeem your story and bring value to all your experiences.

In the midst of humble pilgrims, Parzival is reminded that he needs God. We all need this reminder at some point. It is our connection to eternity that gives us the ability to reconcile our failures and fears to something bigger than ourselves. It is an invitation all humanity needs in order to see how good God actually is. God's goodness is more than an act of eternal duty to His creation. It is an expression of His devotion toward the children He loves. But in order to know for sure, we must get in the mud of our story and allow it to expose what we actually feel about the places we've been, as well as what we think about God Himself.

This is why we need wise elders, men who exist at the fringe of culture, who aren't impressed with our vanity and aren't disappointed in our mistakes. They can hold the tension of our lives, listen to the immature ramblings of a man still in process, and give us space for our questions without attempting to offer answers because they know from experience that if they simply encourage us to keep moving forward on the journey, we will find what we are looking for. They offer us a place to sit in our pain until it has produced the necessary work of transformation within us. They aren't afraid of who we are, and that leaves us in awe because like most men, we long for confidence but feel like frauds.

▼ ▼ ▼

In that place, sacred and strange, Parzival admitted his sorrow to the hermit and told of his many years of wandering. He spoke boldly of his resistance to God and the joy that eluded him like a dream. He spoke of his avoidance of the Church and all things holy, how no priest or prophet would he entertain.

The hermit prodded a little more, speaking of holy things and the nature of God's truth, His salvation, and His Son. He asked Parzival where the root of his sorrow was found. Parzival answered with sincerity and devotion that his two great griefs in this world were that of the Grail and the absence of his wife.

"Longing for your wife makes sense, but if you love her so much, then why are you here?" Trevrizent asked. He gave Parzival no time to respond before continuing, "But as for the Grail, you foolish boy, this cannot be found by mere will. You must be appointed."

186

He went on to say that he himself had seen the Grail and the one it had afflicted, and that the Grail King would never lose his beauty but could not be fully healed, although every week he laid eyes upon the stone. It was that one weekly glance that was keeping him alive—in pain, but alive.

Parzival admitted nothing of having seen the Grail, its king, and its castle as well, his failure locked tight behind his lips, buried in humiliation and grief.

Then the hermit leaned in and said, "Did you know there was a war in heaven? A painful battle between Lucifer and the Trinity that divided heaven itself? And in that place, there was a stone, a stone called the Grail? The battle grew so fierce that the angels who stood on neither side, the 'neutral angels,' removed the stone, along with its incomprehensible and incorruptible power, the source of unimaginable abundance, and brought it down to earth. The tension that resides at the very heart of the Grail is what binds all things together, darkness and light, good and evil, right and wrong, the non-dualistic nature of life itself. If the angels themselves chose one over the other, the power of the Grail would be lost forever. So God has appointed specific defenders to guard the Grail and its potency, an act of service to creation itself. Every Good Friday—today, in fact—a simple dove flies from heaven itself with a small wafer in its mouth that it carries to the stone. When the white wafer comes to rest on the edge of that stone, an inscription appears for just a brief moment, the name of whoever is to serve the Grail. As soon as the name is read, it disappears."

At this point in the story, the hermit's eyes grew heavy with tears. He went on, "The current Grail King is named Anfortas. As a younger man, he longed for power and was driven by lust, so he went out into the world, hunting to fulfill his passion. He came across a pagan knight who had a vision of the true Cross and had gone out searching for some expression of that experience. The two knights' passion and vision collided, and when they did, the Grail King's lance slayed the pagan knight. Yet the pagan knight's lance pierced Anfortas in the groin, leaving a deep wound that requires daily attending. The Grail itself leaves him hanging in the tension of life and death, old age and youth, never fully healed, the only sign of his years the gray in his beard. The land ails because it is out of relationship with the Grail, out of relationship to our great story."

Trevrizent finished, "But recently, there was reason to restore our hope. We received word that there was coming a knight who would ask the question that would heal the king's wound, release him of his duty, and bring the land back into its fullness. Yet on arrival, this youth kept his mouth firmly shut, and the king and our land are left groaning. So now each day Grail knights, the king's attendants, roam the hills in search of that which will combat the stench and pain of his wound, bringing him just a little relief since he is left in such a state. But I see you have had some encounter with these knights, for one of their horses is tied up outside this cave. You have encountered a knight from the Wild Mountain and have stolen his horse. That breed and that saddle give away your misdeeds and what has happened at your hand."

At this, the two men stared deeply into each other's eyes for a long time. Parzival was mortified and could take it no longer. "I was that young man! I am Parzival, son of Gahmuret, who was killed by a lance in a foreign land. I did not steal that horse; I took it from a fallen foe. In my lack of understanding, I did not know from whom I was taking it. I left him the way I left the Red Knight whose armor I bear, whom I killed with sinful hands, Ithir of Kukumerland."

With this, the hermit launched into an assault of information that would reveal the depth of Parzival's failings: "I know who you are. Your actions have brought grief upon your whole family, for you are my nephew. Your mother's brother you have also killed—the Red Knight, whom you were related to, died by your hands. But your iniquity does not end there. Your mother, Herzeloyde, my sister, lies dead in a field near where you left her at your boyhood home, to which there is no return now."

Parzival could not stand it. The grief smashed against him like the waves of the seas upon the shore. It was too much to bear. "God, tell me this is not so!"

"I cannot lie," said the hermit. "Anfortas, the Grail King whom you sat in front of, is my brother as well, your uncle. You have been in the midst of many relatives, Parzival, and you did not even recognize it."

The young man and the holy hermit fell into deep sighs, as though they could take no more. Trevrizent invited Parzival to eat, and they gathered small roots from the ground. Then after tending to his horse, Parzival slept through the night, exhausted from their experience. So it was that Parzival stayed with his uncle, the holy man who lived in the cave at the edge of the wilderness and civility. There, he learned to become a man of prayer, a man of hard work and devotion. He was brought back to Christ in the simplest ways, some of which his mother had given him years before, but in his grief he had abandoned. They came back to him as bread.

Every night the pair sat together, going deeper into the story of the God they served, the story of their lives, and the story of the family from which they came. The Grail in that place became something more to Parzival than simply the redemption of his failure; it became the inner life that strengthened him in ways that no knightly training could provide. He heard more of Anfortas's wound and how the planets and the cold affected it, as well as the relief the king would feel when he fished. That was why Parzival had found him on the lake that night, and why he was also known as the Fisher King.

Parzival learned of the earth and the fracturing that took place when the blood of Abel soaked into it—how that blood still cries out and the innocence lost that day still requires attention. Then, as the hermit talked to him about chivalry and the ways of knighthood, Parzival was transfixed in some ancient way, and the boy within the man was brought back to life. Trevrizent spoke to him in such a way that he was finally able to see that at the very center of chivalry and the chivalric code was not pride and performance, but simple humility of heart. He could see that our greatest successes and most condemning failures both point at the same need for mercy found in us all. It was that tension that the Grail provided for all of creation and that needed restoration.

Parzival's eyes were opened, and in that sacred space healing began and forgiveness was received. As he worked the land, his heart was renewed. After two long weeks, as he prepared to leave, he removed from his body the tunic his mother had given him, letting it lie there in that cave. Some say he made a scarecrow out of it and placed it in the field near the cave where he first gathered roots with his uncle the hermit, Trevrizent.

When Parzival left, he was quiet in his spirit, and his soul had remembered rest, the same rest he had known in the forest as a child. Now, in a forest drenched in rain, he simply picked up where that boy had left off, with openness of heart and holy expectation. He still had his loneliness and longing. He still carried a measure of grief. But he was able to transform that unbearable weight into something he could contain within his frame. He was no longer lost, although he had not ceased from wandering.

▼ ▼ ▼

There is no growth without grief. Grief is simply the unfinished hurt in our hearts that invites us into deeper places of healing and wholeness, asking us to look at something, to feel something we may have been ignoring for years. Not just for the sake of redemption, but for the experience of true comfort. This is what the second Beatitude refers to in Matthew 5:4: "Blessed are those who mourn, for they shall be comforted."

The Gateway to Comfort

Grieving is the gateway to comfort. To ignore grief in our lives, the sadness of our experience, is to set ourselves up for the false comforts offered by culture. This causes us to live in conformity, through addictions and escapism, never being fully awake to the life we've been given. It's when we choose to engage in our grief that we receive comfort from heaven, which I would call hope. This is when our broken pieces reveal parts of a whole image lost to time, perhaps in our own insecurity, and perhaps through our lack of understanding.

David Whyte wrote one of the most beautiful poems about this called "The Well of Grief." He describes grief as more than just an emotion; it is something we sink down into. "Black water," he calls it, where our eyesight is no longer useful and we discover beauty in places where others have only found disappointment, although they "wished for something else."[1]

We can keep wishing for something else, but if we allow ourselves to slide down into the grief of our lives, the experience of what was stolen, what was lost, what was forgotten, then we can do the work necessary to bring care to those moments, those stories. We don't live there; we don't stay in grief forever, lest we end up in depression or lunacy, but it must be engaged and explored. Like initiation, it's an invitation, but it's not optional for those who want to mature and grow into who they were meant to be.

It's time for us to stop wishing for something else and calling it prayer. You and I were given beautiful lives, with unique opportunities nothing like anyone else on planet Earth or in all of eternity. Your life may have similarities to other men's lives, but nothing is exactly the same. You are unique in your experiences, within your circumstances, with your personality, in your family, in your city. From that place, there is "secret water, cold and clear," as Whyte puts it,[2] that you can drink from if you are willing to do this work.

Show up to your life, with all its terrifying specificity, and choose to become a resource to others in their time of need. This is why we weren't meant to do this work of transformation alone. A man typically needs to bring his grief to another man or to a community. We need our grief to be witnessed, shared, and contained. We need the wise elders whom Trevrizent represents, and whom we talked about at length in chapter 7. Wise elders demand that we move forward, and they give us space to do so with care, in a sacred space that seems to whisper to us that anything is possible as they encourage us to stay on the journey and stay in the fight.

In many ways, our childhood is restored in this process. The innocence we once knew is revealed, and much of who we were is brought back into the light. This isn't a demand; it's an invitation to encounter who we were truly meant to be, despite our failures and shortcomings. Each experience we have as we grow older invites us to follow one of two paths. If we choose to ignore or repress our sadness, we will follow the path of anger, which leads to self-destruction. If we choose to engage with our sadness through the work we've been discussing, then we will walk the path of mercy, which leads to self-discovery.

The invitation to show ourselves mercy allows us to offer mercy to others we meet along our journey. You can tell if you have offered yourself mercy by recognizing how other people's brokenness affects you. If you find yourself frustrated with people's emotions, or disappointed when they make poor choices, this might indicate that you're actually frustrated and disappointed with yourself. We can only offer to others that which we think we deserve. If you believe you are worth loving, then you will offer love to others. If you think you deserve judgment, then you will offer the same to others, personally to friends and socially through online comments or criticisms toward people you've never met. This is why the Scriptures exhort us, "Love others as much as you love yourself" (Matthew 22:39 CEV), the second greatest commandment. This doesn't just happen; you have to look in the mirror first.

Why Get You to Cry?

What's the first step of offering yourself mercy and engaging with the sadness in your story? *Tears.*

Look, I'm not interested in getting you to cry as some sort of sensitivity training, or to evaluate your psychological or spiritual health. Tears don't necessarily mean you are healthier in any sense. Tears could very well be a way some people have learned to manipulate others by attempting to make them feel pity. Or if someone has no other emotional tools at his or her disposal, crying becomes the only way to cope with life's circumstances. Neither scenario does an individual any good long-term.

Yet we must not negate the value of tears in our growth journey. Research tells us that tears release oxytocin, the chemical messenger that make us feels connected, at peace, and in love.[3] When we cry, it's a full-body experience emotionally, physically, and spiritually. It's a way to fully engage with who we are and what we're experiencing. When we shed tears with other men, crying connects us in a way that nothing else can. As men, we need to learn to cry with our heads held up. We don't need to put our faces down on our chests, trying to hide or cover the tears. We should lift our heads up, chins pointed to the sky, owning every tear that rolls down our faces. Each one of those tears is counted by God Himself and kept in a bottle (see Psalm 56:8). Our tears have value on earth and in heaven. We cannot ignore them.

I love what Father Richard Rohr says in *From Wild Man to Wise Man*, that "If men are not led through the stages of experiences of grief, which always feels like dying, they end up suffering even more through neurotic pains of aimless depression, desperation, various forms of addiction and even suicidal temptations."[4] Grieving is part of letting go of things we have let lead and define us for far too long. The dysfunctional protection that ignoring grief provided and the version of ourselves that we allowed to exist must die as we move into who we were meant to be. If we don't learn to die in this way, we will feel as if we deserve to die. This is why the suicide rate for men is almost four times what it is for women. The highest suicide rate is among middle-aged white men, who comprise almost 70 percent of all suicides.[5] There was a study done in 2015 on the last words of suicidal men in their notes or recordings before they attempted to take their lives, or succeeded in doing so. The two most common words they used were *useless* and *worthless*.[6]

Men suffer silently, desiring to love and be loved, but they feel inept at fulfilling their role within their home or community. Not only do they feel inept; they are also discouraged by most of society because no one dares say what it means to be a man and not a woman. So men are left not knowing what they uniquely bring to the family unit and to culture as men. This makes a man's grief complex when connected to the ways he already feels as if he has failed and has let down those he loves.

This is why it is so important to make space for grief in a man's life, allowing room for the acceptance of death prior to the experience of it. When Jesus conquered death, it went from being an enemy to an ally. This is how we are supposed to see the seasons and the circumstances in our lives that make us feel as though we are dying. These moments and memories deserve grief. They deserve tears. They deserve the care and containment provided by a wise elder who has gone before us and can walk us through the valley of the shadow. We cannot let our grief turn against us, define us, or even kill us. Instead, we must engage in the work of grief, which helps transform us into the men we were meant to be.

THE WORK

In chapter 5, we approached our grief by identifying where it came from and recognizing how it was affecting us. We learned how to give grief and sadness a space to be experienced and witnessed in our lives. But we cannot remain there; we must learn to move through grief by allowing it to become part of who we are. We do this by letting our pain and failure be our teachers. Everyone's life, no matter how traumatic or horrific their experiences, has something of goodness, or at least of redemption, that can be found, if people are willing to show courage enough to look beyond their pain.

Look at the end of Exodus 3, when the Israelites were leaving their bondage. God says, "Every Israelite woman will ask for articles of silver and gold and fine clothing from her Egyptian neighbors and from the foreign women in their houses. You will dress your sons and daughters with these, stripping the Egyptians of their wealth" (verse 22 NLT). That which oppressed and enslaved you in one season funds and empowers you to walk in freedom in the next. Maybe your life looked like slavery in Egypt, deep in bondage internally and externally, but there is gold to be found in these stories, which must be claimed if we are to walk in who we were meant to be.

We don't want to become slaves to our pain and failures, allowing grief to become guilt. You've been wronged and you've wronged others, but the pain of those moments can teach us how to move forward, if we're willing to make a conscious choice to overcome these experiences through active engagement. The other option is to let them destroy us through shame and self-condemnation.

Here is a simple three-step process to get you started moving forward. Remember to write down your answers in your journal, exploring each step of the exercise as far as you are able.

1. Pick one moment to reflect on. Choose one that marks a wrong done to you or a mistake that has attempted to define you. Write down the details of this experience,

195

and then begin to express what emotions *and* sensations you are experiencing in your body. (Refer to appendix IV for a full "Emotions and Sensations List" to give you a reference, in case you have a difficult time identifying what you are feeling and sensing within your body.) Remember, try not to judge or compare what you're feeling while doing this. If you're unable to explore your own heart and body freely, it will limit your ability to move forward.

2. Ask yourself this question: *What did I learn in that moment?* Regardless of whether it has helped or hindered you in life, you need to be honest and properly assess what it is you took with you from that formative experience. Focus on what beliefs you formed about yourself and others after that experience.

3. Ask yourself: What behavior do I still exhibit today because of the experience I wrote down? Our beliefs directly impact how we behave. If you found a moment in your life that caused deep sadness and taught you to believe that other people weren't safe, and if today you still avoid deep and meaningful connection as a result, that's a powerful piece of information that can do one of two things. It can drive you into regret, or it can empower you to live differently—if you are willing to engage with it. Now ask yourself, *How can I utilize that experience to transform how I live today?* This is a form of reverse engineering your experience to give you positive results from a negative circumstance.

This will take active participation on your part as you continually recognize your desire to avoid connection and the risk of pain. But now you get to make a choice, because you can see these behaviors as part of a belief you no longer want to hold on to. In fact, you can allow the belief that enslaved you in the past to motivate you in the future to write a new story where you discover the beauty of complex relationships that are mutually beneficial.

It takes courage and time, but it is possible to develop new beliefs and form new behaviors. Today you can start, no matter how old you are or how much trauma you've experienced. Hope is just one courageous decision away.

Path 11

Learning to Integrate the Shadow

> Every part of our personality that we do not love will become hostile to us.
>
> Robert Bly, *A Little Book on the Human Shadow*

I have been leading and pastoring in some way both within the Church and parachurch world for over two decades. I thought I was the first in our family line. We all did. My mom and dad didn't know of any priests, ministers, or pastors they could recall in the family, and neither did my living relatives. But that all changed just a handful of years ago. My dad had a few boxes of pictures and random stuff from when my grandfather (his dad) passed away, and Dad hadn't taken time to dig through them until some years later. One day when I was visiting my parents' house, Dad handed me a photocopied newspaper article about my great-great-grandmother. A simple picture of her laughing and smiling ear to ear, with the title "Happier Life for Mrs. Carlton Who Studies the Bible." I didn't know much about her and that side of our family, but within the article she said this: "I've heard my daddy say that his father was a 'hard shell' Baptist preacher and he was a 'primitive' Baptist preacher, that his sons would be Baptists and his grandchildren Methodists!"

When I was growing up, I had my first encounters with Christ and a "calling" within a Baptist church. It happened first in my junior high years, and then in my late teens and early twenties, when I returned and ended up helping plant a church. Not to mention that when my great-great-grandmother says Baptists and Methodists, I hear "the foundation of the Word" and "the leading of the Holy Spirit." This completely represents the ministries I've been involved with, from our Baptist roots to our more charismatic endeavors. In fact, when I finally encountered the Holy Spirit and planted a House of Prayer, the local Methodist church was the first to support and encourage us, while others in the community called us heretics.

I was a seventh-generation pastor and leader in the Church and had no idea until I was in my late thirties and had over fifteen years of experience. I was led by my lineage, the family I didn't know, and that power cannot be minimized.

We are the living embodiment of our ancestors' dreams. Go back just twelve generations, and you are looking at over four thousand people who had to connect, mate, and survive simply for you to exist. You are not a mistake; your story is not random. You could have been born into any family, in any city, at any time in human history, but you were chosen for this time and this place, with a specific story and set of circumstances that would bring God the greatest glory, if you would turn toward Him.

Your lineage may have been hidden from you for some purpose that must be uncovered. You may be looking at situations in your life and may have predetermined, *This cannot be God. No good can come from this, and there's no way He can use any of it.* But the truth of the matter is that you don't need to pray it away; you don't need to forget about it. You need to engage with it.

Doing this doesn't mean everything you've experienced is good or "happened for a reason." That would be an awful thing to say to someone who is experiencing or has experienced deep trauma. We must understand that there are experiences in our life that are just painful, just wrong, just blatantly other people's abuse of their free will toward us. But that doesn't mean God cannot do something with it. He wastes nothing and has a long history of creating beauty from ashes and life from death. There is something in your line that can be redeemed, if you are willing to do the work that no one else was willing to do before you.

It's broken and beautiful; it's tension and mystery. It's the way God designed it. You can feel it within you. It's why you're reading this book, pursuing health and growth, feeling frustrated one moment and expectant the next. It's why you're searching and stumbling. You recognize that there's something missing, there's something that isn't right, and you can't quite put your finger on it. I believe the old myths were right and there's a part of us that went into exile when we were born. Martin Shaw calls it the "Wild Twin." Other religions might term it the divine twin, or maybe it's part of what Jung called the shadow, or what Robert Bly tells us is in "the long bag we drag behind us."[1] I don't know what you call it, but there's a part of us that we must reconcile to ourselves if we're going to become who we were meant to be.

So many men see the potential within themselves, the opportunity and beauty in their story. So they start a business, a family, further education, or a spiritual pursuit, but they soon find themselves sabotaging those pursuits because they cannot trust what's being presented. They become scared or frustrated and aren't willing to take the risks necessary to grow their lives in a way that allows them to reach their full potential. They can feel the twin within them; they know the twin exists. But they won't reconcile with that part of themselves. So they self-destruct in a hundred different ways and lose the momentum life was offering, sometimes "in the name of the Lord" because in fear they offer things to God He never asked for.

The goal is wholeness, to integrate the shadow parts of who we are, some of which we didn't know existed. We do this by moving forward with our work of transformation, uncovering in ourselves what others are running from. This is not a distraction in our life; it's an invitation.

▼ ▼ ▼

The rain struck Parzival's face, and the air felt fresh and alive. An alchemical reaction between body and soul made the whole world come alive. He traversed the landscape with a renewed sense of wonder and expectation, and for a brief moment the world seemed to make sense.

But that moment was not to last long. He happened across a lonely knight who in turn drew arms against him. This didn't bring Parzival the usual thrill of battle and rush of impending victory. Something had changed within him. There was a peace he had never known, which he didn't want to depart from. Sorrow and grief filled his heart as he lowered his lance at the thought that he might be losing something beautiful he had just found.

The two knights charged and fought with fierceness, not yet recognizing the friend in each other. They delivered blows with spears and lances that splintered, until these gave way to swords. Each blow thundered like a mighty hammer. Parzival's opponent was steadily being overthrown and was about to give in, when, in a good turn of events, a young page who had come along with the opposing knight recognized Parzival's coat of arms and shouted, "It's Parzival! Gawain, it's Parzival!"

Hearing this, Parzival threw his sword far from him and released Gawain, in great sorrow that he had fought someone he held so dear. Gawain, worn out from battle, fell back into the page's arms and told Parzival that there was no need for sorrow in a moment like this. He admitted that their violence had gotten the best of him, and that in some way it was always bound to be. Gawain stood and embraced Parzival in the fullness of the strength he had left, exhausted from battle. He began to tell him of his adventures and how Cundry had spoken to him harshly as well, and sent him into a great quest that included castles full of damsels under enchantment, and also a castle of marvels.

In a series of events we won't take time here to unfold, Gawain had found himself on a collision course with another king and had mistaken Parzival for that king in his haste for battle. He informed Parzival that Arthur and the other Knights of the Round Table were near. They had come to behold the battle that was about to ensue, and Parzival should go join them.

▼ ▼ ▼

As Parzival begins his journey toward redemption and restoration, he encounters an unknown knight who is revealed to be Gawain, a brother in arms, not an adversary. Initially, Parzival has no idea what he's fighting or why, but he knows that this force is distracting and deterring him from where he's headed. A large part of Wolfram's telling of this story is dedicated to Gawain and his quest, which led to the castle of marvels, many women, and tales of great heights of passion and eros. I've left that out in our telling to stay more concise and focused, but within this tale and many others we see what Gawain represents—the "Lover" archetype. This Lover is an archetype found within all men. It must be wrestled with in order for us to grow into maturity. If we don't engage it, the Lover will keep large portions of who we are in immaturity throughout our lives.

The Four Archetypes within a Man

Within genders, an archetype is a reoccurring thought process or behavior pattern that occurs unconsciously within an individual. These archetypes can be immature or mature, healthy or unhealthy, depending on a person's experience. But each archetype requires specific care and development to grow into its fullness. The Lover is one of the four archetypes described and explored in many psychological studies, but most famously in the book *King, Warrior, Magician, Lover* by Robert Moore and Douglas Gillette. The *King* represents the part of a man that either remains a selfish, entitled prince or grows into a generative, powerful King who is decisive, creates order, holds fast to his integrity, and puts others before himself.

The *Warrior* is the part of a man that, in its immaturity, turns to violence and rage, seeking to earn praise through competition and exploits. But the mature Warrior keeps his aggression in check and utilizes it to fuel his purpose as he remains focused, adaptable, loyal, and disciplined.

The *Magician* archetype (if you don't like the word *Magician*, I often change it to the title of *Priest*), in its immaturity, becomes a manipulative know-it-all. But in his maturity, the Magician is a resourceful, spiritual, wise guide who sees the world in nondualistic beauty. He brings things together that other men would never consider, for the purpose of mastering his world and becoming a resource to his community.

But the *Lover* is our focus. The Lover archetype, in its immaturity, is addicted to anything that will turn him on or numb him out. He uses other people for his benefit, regardless of their feelings. His emotions are the priority and usually take up a lot of space. Yet the mature Lover is deeply empathetic and carries an awakened spirituality within him because all the world feels alive to him at every level—taste, touch, sight, smell, sound. This isn't just about sexuality; it's about arousal. Arousal is that which brings us into a fully alive and engaged state where we're attuned and attentive to the moment we're in and the people we're with.

The Lover archetype within a man is about connection and engagement with the world around him. It's about maintaining and exploring that rush of desire, even sensuality, but it must be formed and sharpened through the tempering of care and containment. It's the mature Lover's passion that unites the other archetypes together. It pulls the King into his integrity, the Warrior into his focus, and the Magician (Priest) into his reflective study.

Gawain is the mythological symbol of the Lover in Arthurian legends. He's the handsome ladies' man who is in touch with his emotions and isn't afraid to utilize these skills, wavering between maturity and immaturity when engaging the feminine. He's a fierce knight, full of courage and chivalry. But in stories like Gawain and Lady Ragnell, or Gawain and the Green Knight, we find him in touch with his emotions, able to sweep women off their feet as they fall madly in love with him and his gallantry.

This is what Parzival is going to battle against as he begins his return journey, and so it is with all men. The first thing we must redeem is connection to our emotion, to the world around us, and to the beauty of our sexuality. But most of this doesn't feel masculine anymore because it is less about passion and purpose and more about romanticism. We still find ourselves in the reverberations of the romantic era, which tell us "it's all about what you feel," and "if it feels good, it must be God," and "anything that's difficult or frustrating and requires sacrifice [and dare we say suffering?], reject and run from as if it were the devil himself."

This kind of thinking has invaded every aspect of the churches we attend and the culture we engage with daily. It's about comfort and conformity, not redemption and maturity. When we attend church, we expect the chairs to be nice, the sermon to be relevant, the temperature to be consistent, the music to be easy and repeatable. And the people should all be morally acceptable in order to participate. These concepts are birthed from romantic ideals that were a fad and have now become a foundation in our society.

The Mature Lover's Emotions

The Lover archetype in its fullness, however, isn't about being led by emotion and making decisions based on how we feel in the moment. The mature Lover recognizes his emotions, explores them, and gives them their proper place in the correct time. He does not allow them to be the center of how he connects with others or how he engages in the world around him. The mature man, engaged with the Lover archetype, knows how to have an emotion, define that emotion and where it's coming from, and then decide if this is a proper time to explore or express that emotion. He can decide whether or not he needs to place it somewhere for the time being so he can engage with it at a later time because his strength and steadfast devotion are required in this moment, not his feelings.

This is a huge distinction for men who want to grow into maturity. Notice I didn't say that they ignore their emotions. Doing that would still be an expression of immaturity. They understand that their emotions have value, so they place what they're experiencing in a journal or text a friend so they can revisit an emotional moment at a more appropriate time, with men who can provide a level of care and containment for what they've experienced.

Reengaging with the Lover part of himself gives a man back his tenderness and sensitivity without making him weak or a pushover. In the masculine expression, to remain sensitive and tender is about physical and spiritual awareness, a way of being that allows a man to fully engage his empathy with courage. We see this in Jesus as He weeps over Jerusalem and prays in the Garden before His crucifixion. We can also find it in Paul's description of love in 1 Corinthians 13, when he says, "Love bears all things, believes all things, hopes all things, endures all things" (verse 7).

The Lover doesn't avoid pain; he is keenly aware of it and chooses to embrace it anyway. We cannot afford to numb ourselves to this part of our experience. The masculine Lover has made an agreement with the reality that part of real love is pain and sacrifice.

This is why marriage is never about your happiness. It's about your holiness, your development, your character. Of course we will have joy, but it's found in the journey and is no longer circumstantial. We wrestle and struggle, fully awake and fully engaged in the seasons of our relationship, having empathy and a mature emotional expression that allows our spouse to recognize where we are and what we're experiencing. In this way, sex becomes a sacrament and not a demand, a reminder of the love we share, and part of the dialogue and dance we develop within our commitment to one another.

Little Room for the Lover

Christianity has very little room for the Lover and has been known for persecuting this expression in men because it is feared. It is defined only as lust, condemning any form of healthy sensuality and sexuality that attempts to find its way into conversation. Your body as a man was designed to seek arousal and sensual pleasure. There is absolutely nothing wrong with that; it simply needs proper care and definition, not avoidance and rejection.

Just look at Song of Songs, a full book of the Bible dedicated to the healthy display of erotic love in poetic verse. Sure, it could contain allegorical imagery pertaining to Christ and His Bride, and how He loves and pursues her. But that's not its entire purpose. If it were, why is the book so sexually charged? Those who relegate such a beautiful book about sexual expression only to allegory reveal their own fear and brokenness toward the subject, not everyone else's.

I am in no way denying the disturbing reality that every human on earth struggles with inappropriate sexual thoughts, feelings, and behaviors that are in direct conflict with God's original intent. I am simply offering you an alternative to repressing your sexual leadings by stating that they deserve honor and honesty, and the proof is this beautiful and often overlooked book in the Old Testament. We need this book to remind us of the celebration of sex and sexuality, while remembering God's desire for us to "be holy as He is holy" (see 1 Peter 1:15–16). These statements are not in conflict; they are in agreement. We get one with the other, not despite it.

This is what Parzival is wrestling with, and what we are wrestling with as men. We don't even know it, so we make it about something else. This has never been about how much sex you get in your marriage or how much you masturbate. Men's sexuality is being domesticated by pornography. Porn is not about exploration or curiosity; it's actually training your imagination to believe fantasy should be reality. Many single men engaging in regular porn consumption find it hard to stay deeply connected in relationships and even harder to stay faithful in those relationships. This is why many of these men shy away from the commitment of marriage.

Married men who regularly look at porn either lose desire for their spouse (because it's easier to look at their screens) or their expectations of sex put unhealthy pressure on their spouse to perform in ways these men have seen on the Internet. This eventually deteriorates trust and intimacy within the marriage.[2] Porn develops an unhealthy fantasy that many men are choosing so they can live outside reality, instead of wrestling with awkward emotions and arousal toward a woman they are attracted to (or married to) and learning to deny themselves and struggle toward the intimacy they long for. Instead of utilizing courage, they choose porn and embrace cowardice, hiding behind screens, masturbating to images of women they've never met.

Many men's sensual imaginations have been colonized this way by fake images and videos that stir up the Lover's immature side rooted in addiction or impotence because of a lack of connection to reality. This allows a large percentage of men to disconnect from their emotions and experiences, leaving them filled with shame. And shame has been telling their story ever since.

But it doesn't have to be that way. We can stop being afraid of our emotions and our sexuality by embracing them, engaging with them, discussing them with other men and finding within them their redemptive purpose in our lives. We have to begin to believe that our emotions are trying to tell us something, and it's time we listened. Let the pain of those emotions and our sexual brokenness tell us what they're actually looking for. It's not expression and orgasm; it's care and kindness. These cycles of shame are robbing us of the conviction and passion that will move our story forward into the full redemptive purposes we were created for. We can find our joy again by playfully engaging and experiencing that which we previously ignored and repressed. We are not adding weight to our lives, but rather relief due to the fact that we don't have to spend so much energy burying what's there. Instead, we can develop a language and lifestyle that make room for all of it, lived out in mature and godly choices rather than shame.

▼ ▼ ▼

Little did the knights know that in the nearby inlet just offshore, a great warrior had anchored his ship, along with another twenty-five ships from his fleet. A foreign land's army was approaching with excitement and anticipation, and neither Parzival, nor Gawain, nor even Arthur himself was aware of it. This great warrior began exploring the local area personally, scouting and searching, for what we don't know. But he was resplendent in his armor, more brilliant than most would ever see in their lifetime. Gold and jewels of all manner adorned his knightly vestments, making him shine in the sun like an angelic force of nature or the otherworld.

Parzival was the first to spot this warrior, and he again felt a tinge of sorrow at having to face that which he was so desperately trying to avoid since his time with Trevrizent. Yet he wasted no time confronting the magnificent warrior. They lowered their lances and began to charge, but within Parzival it was clear something had changed. Perhaps for the first time, part of him realized it could be his death he was facing. They ran their horses at one another, javelins exploding as they met, splinters falling to the ground like snow.

The mysterious knight was astonished. Never before had he encountered a knight with his javelin who remained mounted upon his steed. In Parzival, he knew he was dealing with someone whose strength matched or exceeded his own. They fought and fought, but neither could gain an advantage from horseback. Each of their mighty horses tired before the knights did, so the riders jumped off to the ground, ready to pursue and overpower each other. The foreign knight shouted "Thabronit!" as he ran into battle—the name of his home.

Parzival had never experienced what he was now encountering. The power, ferocity, and desire of this warrior was giving him his first taste of defeat, completely overwhelming him on the battlefield. But he thought of his bride, Condwiramurs, and how he longed to see her again. He thought of family, of children, and of God. In his devotion, he prayed as the two men thrashed one another in the beating sun.

A whirlwind of skill and aggression, these men were committed to the end. After several strategic blows, Parzival lunged forth to seize an opportunity for advantage and swung his sword directly upon the warrior's helmet with all the strength remaining within him. To his astonishment and horror, his sword shattered. Both warriors fell to the ground, stunned at what had just transpired. The sword young Parzival had acquired through immaturity from slaying his own uncle, Ithir, the Red Knight, was left in pieces. It could no longer help him where he was now headed. Both men jumped to their feet, Parzival left at a disadvantage, a broken sword in hand.

The foreign knight finally spoke: "I have never faced another knight quite like you, and it seems that you are willing to meet your end. But what honor would it bring me if I took the life of an unarmed man? In fact, if your sword had not broken, I think you would have taken me. Come, let us catch our breath and make a truce."

There they sat, in full armor, beneath the sun in a grass field so peaceful you would never have imagined what had taken place there moments before. The foreigner spoke again: "My name is Feirefiz of Angevin. I preside over many lands and much wealth."

Immediately, the untamed face of Cundry invaded Parzival's mind. The words she had spoken before Arthur's court came back to him: "You have a brother, a magpie-skinned warrior from Angevin; you are both sons of Gahmuret." He asked him, "Would you remove your helmet so I can see your features? I promise no harm will come to you."

The foreigner said he had no fear since Parzival had no sword and his own was so readily available. Even if Parzival were to try something, he would cut him down where he sat. So he pulled his helmet off and revealed his marbled skin, like a magpie, black and white. It was Parzival's brother.

Parzival removed his own helmet in excitement and shouted, "You are kin to me! My father is Gahmuret. I am Parzival, your brother!"

The two embraced, and great joy filled their whole beings. Any exhaustion that had followed them from their battle evaporated as they laughed and cried in that place. Feirefiz said that he was searching for their father, and it was Parzival who had to give him the news of the Dark Knight's death in battle in a foreign land. So it was that Feirefiz went looking for a father and found a brother instead.

▼ ▼ ▼

We are at war with the parts of ourselves we never knew existed, the part left in a foreign land, so to speak, because it didn't get us the affection and affirmation we needed to survive. We have parts of ourselves that have gone into exile by our own hand, and they must be encountered and integrated as we walk toward redemption and full maturity.

You can spend your whole life fighting these hidden versions of yourself, going blow for blow, but you stay the same person. There's no forward momentum in a battle like this. It's no wonder so many men feel tired and beaten down, with no relief and no rest. We go to war with ourselves, fighting the parts we don't understand or we consider "dangerous" to ourselves and others—our sexuality, our humor, our aggression, our creativity, and so much more.

All of these are forced out in the name of being responsible, and being presentable to those who have attempted to provide care and guidance for us. These guides didn't want us to be who we are, but who they needed us to be. It wasn't their fault, and it wasn't ours. It's part of undealt-with trauma that keeps us in these cycles, controlled and neutered, so others don't have to be afraid of us. We keep attempting to be "good," and the moralistic legalism that protected us when we were young gives way to manipulating and exerting control over others in our adult life.

Then, when we see an opportunity to move to gain an advantage, we take it. In all our zeal to move forward, however, to end the cycles that have frustrated our lives, to be done with this part of our story, we don't kill the part of us that's in the way. Instead, our sword breaks against it, as Parzival's broke against his unrecognized brother. The weapon that got us here, the thing we gained through our immature behavior, no longer works. Like a broken sword, it lies in a pile in front of us. The cycle ends when the thing that has gotten us this far is destroyed. All our vain attempts at behavior modification, religious activity, serial monogamy, and destructive discipline couldn't get us where we longed to be. Our vain efforts are gone; there's no way to get them back. Then the invitation comes to us from somewhere deep and ancient within: "Come and rest, and catch your breath."

The One Life You Could Save

The answer is simple and so frustrating. We want it to be black and white, good or bad, right or wrong, one or the other. Instead, we find out in the end that it's marbled, it's magpie. And it's in that tension, that mystery between beauty and brokenness, danger and promise, where we find what we've always been looking for—home.

Look at the beginning and ending lines of Mary Oliver's powerful poem "The Journey." She begins, "One day you finally knew / What you had to do . . ." And she ends, " . . . Determined to do / The only thing you could do, Determined to save / The only life you could save."[3]

In my opinion, you are the one life you could save. You only have control over you, and you are worth fighting for. You cannot fix your marriage, your friendships, your kids, or anyone else. You can simply become the best version of you a little more each day in front of those you love, and you can become the inspiration that invites them into the same work.

We have to let go of our eagerness to save everyone and everything. That's not compassion or love; that's ego. You cannot save everyone. In truth, you cannot save anyone. Your life simply becomes a resource that others can learn and glean from on their journey as we all head toward home, toward Eden.

I love what one of my friends always used to say: "I am just one beggar telling another beggar where he got his bread." We share what we have with kindness and mercy, and in that sharing, people feel loved and seen and celebrated. When they ask where we got our joy, our peace, our hope, we can point them toward home and toward the Father. But we must learn to do the work of integration, which is the power of resurrection in our everyday experiences, bringing life to that which we thought was dead and gone. Integration is not just about *knowing* your story, it's about *learning* from your story, gaining from your story, and moving forward in the fullness of your story. There will be difficult days, and there will be days filled with supernatural potential, but we just place one foot in front of the other and learn to enjoy the journey.

You are the sum total of all your experiences, and so much more. Whoever you are, wherever you find yourself, you are enough.

THE WORK

Revisit your story map and your genogram, both of which you did earlier, and see what parts of you may have been abandoned or rejected. (If you skipped doing these important exercises, visit appendix II and appendix III and catch up on that vital work now.)

I want you to look back through these tools and begin to see if you can uncover some of your shadow parts that have been lost along the way. Was it the childlike part of you that was told to grow up too fast? Was it the adventurous part of you that was told to sit still? Or maybe the romantic, emotional side of you that was told boys don't cry? What was thrown away that needs to be redeemed and integrated back into who you are today?

Ask yourself this: *Am I being the truest version of myself, or am I acting like an imposter to appease others?*

We need to know the answer to this question so that we can clearly define the hidden parts of ourselves that we are tempering and learning to redeem. Otherwise, we are rejecting the truest parts of who we are—a form of rejection that leaves us anxious, fearful, depressed, or angry at our loss.

This week show up to the life you've been given in a way you have not before. There is hope in these stories, grace in the experiences, and love far beyond the shame we have known.

Path 12

Arriving Where You Always
Belonged

> True humility, we believe, consists of two things. The first
> is knowing our limitations. And the second is getting the
> help we need.
>
> Robert Moore, *King, Warrior, Magician, Lover*

Every person who encountered the living Christ left with more
questions than answers. This wasn't meant to introduce confusion; it was an invitation on Jesus' part. Jesus never said "worship Me," never said "read your Scriptures," never said "make
sure you go to meetings." He simply said, "Follow Me." It was
an otherworldly calling to the Kingdom, spoken about only in
poetic mythology we call parables, stories that drew us beyond
the borders of our modern sanctums, into the divine realm.

Such broad and mysterious language tempers the ego. You
can't quantify it, examine it under a microscope, or dissect it
in a lab. There are no formulas, and there is not one person
on planet Earth in all of history with perfect theology, not one

church, one preacher, or one denomination. We all see in part, and that has been the divine plan all along, so we would humble ourselves in service to something greater than ourselves.

When we dive into the space of the Grail Castle, the space where past, present, and future meet, all timelines go out the window there, and modern definitions of success go with them. In places like this, we realize that we are not the center. Our ego has falsely led us to unhelpful places within our psyche and within our culture, and has offered us versions of success that trap us in unrelenting cycles of disappointment, shame, and guilt. Real transformation begins when we stop fighting the shadow, as we talked about in the previous chapter, and start killing our ego.

Changing Our Definition of Success

We have become obsessed with creating quick fixes and easy answers for complex problems, but they haven't served us well. In a culture of "Amazon Basics" and counterfeits, people settle for whatever is cheapest, whatever is fastest. It doesn't matter if it's quality or if it will last; people simply want what will fill the need now—and it must be delivered same day, or I don't want it. That's why fast-food religion is so appealing and spirituality is relegated to the radicals, the monastic, or the priests. Fast-food religion is what we chase if we are afraid of hell. True spirituality is what we chase if we have been through hell.

Our definition of success changes as we are set free from the taskmaster of an ego-centered life. Whatever you've determined success looks like, you will pursue with your whole heart. Our definition of success is what drives our values, our purpose, and our worth. But we have to realize that our success isn't found in what we do, but rather in who we become, and we were meant to become something very specific.

The lie that you can be anything you want has made its way into every area of culture and the Church. It's a core belief of Western civilization, or at least of Americans. "I can be anything!" "I can do anything!" Yet that has led to great disillusionment and frustration for young people who thought a positive attitude and a great social media presence would allow them to "follow their dreams" and become independently wealthy by the ripe old age of seventeen. Instead of being formed and initiated, young men are coddled and compromised, without leadership and wise elders to guide them into models of success that offer greater joy than money, greater influence than fame, and greater legacy than platforms and positions.

But to truly succeed, you have to be willing to stay in it until the end. You can't give up. You aren't allowed to quit. You have to keep going, regardless of how difficult the road ahead is. When others fall off, you forge ahead, asking questions, embracing mystery and tension, and finding ways of existing that others have never experienced.

▼ ▼ ▼

Parzival mentioned to his newfound brother that Arthur was near and was expecting him, and they immediately went to see the great king. They were greeted with much honor and affection. Both were invited to sit at the Round Table as Arthur's beloved Knights. All the court was dazzled at Parzival's brother's beauty, his wealth, and his grace. Feirefiz and Parzival told many stories of quests and adventure, and everyone marveled in awe at all that had transpired, including Arthur, Lord of the Britons.

The celebration and its daring tales were only broken when a woman on horseback rode into the circle. She was beautifully clothed in a black hood decorated with a flock of turtledoves wrought in gold alongside the Grail's insignia. She quickly dismounted and knelt before Parzival. Even with her face obscured and covered, all could hear her weeping.

Parzival knew immediately who this was and felt a flush of great anger. In her grieving, however, she asked him for a pardon's kiss and received what she came for. As she did, she leapt to her feet and threw off her shroud and hood in the center of the circle. Cundry, the great Grail defender, was now fully revealed.

She praised Parzival and then spoke these words: "Be joyful, yet be restrained. The dove has come again, and your name has been revealed upon the Grail. All hail, all hail, the new ruler of the Grail!"

She informed Parzival that his wife had been with child when he departed, and that Condwiramurs and their twin sons were now headed to Grail Castle as well, so they needed to leave immediately. He could bring one man with him if he so desired, so he turned to his brother. Without a word, Feirefiz agreed, and they were on their way.

That's how it went, the brothers and the great Grail defender side by side on redemption's road. King Arthur himself blessed their journey and sent out word:

> The Grail no man had ever
> acquired by forced endeavor,
> Save he whom God gave its command.
> This word went out to every land:
> By force the Grail one cannot win.
> This taught men never to begin
> The Holy Grail by force to get.[1]

As they drew close to the castle, a strong force of knights rode out toward them. They recognized from Cundry's dove insignia that these approaching three meant only good. Feirefiz tried to stir his brother into action, spurring him to attack the knights, but in a flash Cundry seized the reins of both men and stopped them in their tracks. She spoke with authority, saving them from their own immaturity: "In a moment, you will look upon their banners and shields and recognize that these are Grail Knights. They are ready to serve you, not attack you."

Parzival, taken aback by his own impetuous nature, knew that he still needed to be led and asked Cundry to lead them from that moment on to the Grail Castle. This great trickster led two great warriors ahead of the company of Grail Knights as they resumed their journey toward redemption.

▼ ▼ ▼

Redemption is the heart of the Father. We are never so far gone that we can't humbly be brought back into right relationship with God. All our problems may not disappear. Our marriage may still need time to heal. Our children may need more opportunity to forgive. Our friends may not want to be around, or may never come back at all. We may be broken, busted, and beat down. But it all will leave us in a position to receive that which is greater than any earthly position or possession we could acquire. Having forgotten our woes and found the Source, we have found our family, our tribe, our purpose, a new definition of what it means for us to be centered or whole. Our identity has been redeemed as the core of who we truly are is revealed.

Led Where We Always Belonged

Men need moments like this—to see themselves and be received as they are, as who they knew they were all along, even though they lost track of it somehow along the way. It is confirmation alongside affirmation, in the midst of those we respect, that launches us into our second half of life as wise elders to young men who would follow and who need the sharp edge of initiation to bring them into right relationship with God and with themselves.

So this is where we are, a Grail Trinity—a spirit-being of deep conviction (Cundry), a son from a foreign land (Feirefiz), and a father who has wandered into all the right places to find his way back to family (Parzival). These are the protectors of the Grail, forging forward with a dangerous old woman leading the way, powerful and confident, leading the men into their proper position, serving the Grail. This divine trio isn't serving one another, but something greater. And there's no time to argue about female and male gender roles when your focus is the Grail, when your eyes are fixed on God.

This is important to recognize in a world that wants to jump to quick definitions and false assumptions about how a man and a woman serve one another in a home and marriage as we develop a life together. The great and powerful Grail defender, Cundry, in all her convicting language, saw the change in Parzival, and it was undeniable. So she led them to where they always belonged.

I love this image because I would not be the man I am today without my wife. She has spoken with me so directly in certain seasons that it was undeniable that God was speaking through her. It felt harsh at the time, but it was necessary. In seasons as we grow together both in age and in wisdom, there will be times when she leads the way and times when I lead the way. But our focus is always Jesus, the center of it all.

▼ ▼ ▼

Once the company arrived at Grail Castle, they moved immediately to the main hall and into the presence of the Grail King. There, the procession was already in motion. The golden cups were filled, the lanterns were brought out, the lamps were lit, the bleeding lance displayed, the maidens present—it was all just like the first time Parzival had been there.

This time, however, the great king spoke with a new boldness, an assurance he had not had before: "I have waited a long time for my suffering to end. When you left me last time, I was grieved that this might not come to be. But if you are Parzival, then 'All hail to you,' and do this thing for

222

me. I beg you to ask these knights and maids to keep me from looking upon the Grail for seven nights and eight days, so then I can surely die."

Parzival began to weep with his whole body. He shook, and his shoulders gave way as tears streamed down his face. He had never known a grief like this. He wept for himself. He wept for his Uncle Anfortas, the Grail King. He wept for his bride, the earth he had forsaken, all the family he had met along the way. He wept for God's grace that brought him back to the place of his failure, even though he knew full well he didn't deserve it. He knelt before the Grail in reverence of God and the Trinity. But then he stood at full height, never once dropping his chin to chest. With every eye and every soul and every heartbeat in the hall aimed right on him, he asked with gentle speech and a full voice, "Dearest uncle, whom does the Grail serve?"

▼ ▼ ▼

He didn't learn this question from someone, but from bearing the weight of his journey, and this question has only one answer: the Grail serves the king who serves it, whose lineage Parzival was part of. Parzival was the only son in the family line who could take the throne, the only living heir of the Grail King. His whole life had led him to value the family he had lost, the family he had slain, the family he had abandoned. Yes, God had "called" him through the symbolism of the dove, the wafer that touched the stone, and Parzival's name appearing on the Grail. But how much of our calling is actually God's invitation to participate in the redemption of our family lines by living in the fullness of what they could never attain?

This one moment was for Parzival a conscious, humbling choice to return to the family he had run from, for the sake of something greater than his own ego. Remember the mother who died of heartbreak when he left (Herzeloyde), the grieving cousin he met on the road and tried to avoid (Sigune), the uncle he killed and whose armor he stole (Ithir, the Red Knight), the

223

wife and children he abandoned to pursue his own adventures (Condwiramurs and the twins), the uncle in the cave who called him back to God (Trevrizent). And now, lying before him, was the Grail King (Anfortas), his uncle, suffering because Parzival had been too immature to understand how to engage with his own family and the profound impact of their suffering.

The course correction being offered to Parzival in this moment, even though he had failed and stumbled the first time, the very reason he was able to ask the question now, was that he was finally able to see that all he had experienced and overcome was about family and legacy, not ego and conquest. The question wasn't just *from* him, it was *for* the redemption of his entire family line. Just one person in the midst of a family line who chooses to live differently and pay the price can change generations of abuse and brokenness.

This is why we do StoryWork, a tool we use in our ministry the Fight.[2] This is why we embrace the suffering, the sacrifice, and the circumstances of our lives. As we embrace who we are, we discover who we were always meant to be within our family and within eternity itself. Parzival was now invited to do in wholeness what his uncle had rejected in woundedness. You can't learn this in a classroom; you can't read it in a book. No one can hand this to you. You must go searching; you must go do the work.

The question I have chosen for this version of the story is from Chrétien's version of the story. The question in Wolfram's version is "Dearest Uncle, what is it that ails you?" Both questions are the same. One focuses on the body, and the other focuses on the family. Only when we have suffered do we finally have empathy for those who are suffering. Only when we have experienced the loss of family do we begin to long for it. Only when we are able to see and embrace our own frailty do we yield to God in such a way that it rewrites generations of brokenness.

This is why it's about a question and not simply answering a riddle. If it were just a riddle, you could search for the right answer. But if you have to find the right question, you must become the right person first. The right question will always lead you to the right answer.

▼ ▼ ▼

The change was powerful and instant. The Grail King's body was transformed immediately, and beauty shown straight out of him, dwarfing every other beauty Parzival had ever seen. It had a holy source. The presence of the divine entered, and all bent their heads and wept. A question so simple was a doorway to the very heavens themselves. The hall seemed lit by an inner light. The king, the cripple, wasn't forced to die in waiting. He was healed. This was a beauty beyond court grandeur, beyond earthly wealth; this was the healing of the very soul. And it shown out in every direction from the east, the west, the north, and the south—all felt and received the reverberation of this moment.

In that instant and every instant since, Parzival himself was recognized as the Grail Lord. In the midst of this great light, his wife and his two sons came into the room, and the family struck out toward one another. Although Parzival and Condwiramurs longed for a full embrace, he gently touched his wife's shoulder, and then her cheek, and stared deeply into her eyes. Every year they had missed each other fell away to the floor. He gracefully pulled her closer, and for a long time, a sweet time, secret things were said between them—some fierce, some harsh, but all with love in the two hearts. All the pain they had endured, the separation and the abandonment, were dealt with right there in the presence of that great light.

When the twin boys couldn't take it anymore, they finally invaded the space of our two lovers, pouncing on their father like little lion cubs. Tears splashed everywhere they looked. The exhaustion of the journey and the happiness in his heart overwhelmed our hero. He fell onto the couch, into the deepest sleep he had ever known. He had traversed a

225

thousand difficulties, had peered into the mystic, had made all the right mistakes, and had been honored by the greatest knights this world has ever seen. Yet here in this warm space, with his wife and his children, the man finally knew peace.

▼ ▼ ▼

We don't have the space to fully elaborate here on how the rest of the story unfolds. There aren't enough pages left to tell you about how Parzival's brother got married and baptized, and then became an evangelist to the East. There isn't enough time left in these pages to tell you of the great adventures Parzival had with his two sons, nor of the love that continued to grow between him and his bride as they wept, laughed, and loved all through a great many years later. It might also bring you too much sorrow to read about the death of Sigune and how she was buried next to the husband she had mourned all those years. The further adventures of Anfortas, Trevrizent, Gawain, and even King Arthur himself must be left for another time and other stories. For now, we will end with this:

▼ ▼ ▼

Parzival finally fell into a deep, restful slumber, the likes of which had evaded him for many years. A fire was roaring in the hearth, and his children were content, asleep around his feet. His wife, Condwiramurs, however, the woman who had married him for love, was wide awake. Safe in his arms and secure in his embrace, from that place she watched through a great window the sun rising on a brand-new day.

▼ ▼ ▼

Our story may have come to an end, but Parzival's life, like ours, will have plenty more quests and questions. But for now, there are no arms to pick up, no swords or shields or great battles. Like Parzival, we also have found the object of our affection. It isn't happiness, but service to the Grail—to God. And the question is the answer. Whom does the Grail serve? Well, of course it serves the Grail King. Who is the Grail King? It is now Anfortas's nephew, Parzival. Not just the Parzival in our story, but the Parzival in each of us. The part of us that has chosen something more than what the world has offered, something more than our disappointment and failures.

In fact, it's our great disappointments and failures that have led us here, that have led us back home. We have "made all the right mistakes," and they have made us who we are today. You don't have to run from what you've done or the places you've been. You don't have to be afraid to search your story for the things that have formed you into who you are today. Something within those experiences will show you the path of redemption and will reveal the power of resurrection, for those who have eyes to see and ears to hear.

The Center of the Story

In the Passover celebration, there is a beautiful parallel to the images provided here. At the Seder meal, once the youngest child has drunk from the cup, he must ask his father the meaning of this whole experience: What is the purpose, what is the point? Then the father recounts the entire story of the people of Israel and their exodus from Egypt. We find the reference to this in Exodus 12:25–27:

> "And when you come to the land that the LORD will give you, as he has promised, you shall keep this service. And when your children say to you, 'What do you mean by this service?' you shall say, 'It is the sacrifice of the LORD's Passover, for he passed over the houses of the people of Israel in Egypt, when he struck the Egyptians but spared our houses.'"

227

There seems to be a direct connection between "Whom does the Grail serve?" in Parzival's story and "What do you mean by this service?" in the Passover. Both questions are an opportunity to recount what has brought you here in the first place. What devotion and deliverance have made a way for you? It's not just a moment; it's a memorial, a ritual, a remembrance that we are not the center of the story, He is. God has always been and always will be the center of the story. He is not just holding together creation and leading us through our story; He is reality itself hidden within every moment, every person, and everything we encounter. He is goodness and light, life and death, judge and friend, merciful and abundant in His grace. His goal is always love.

For men, the value of initiation and the telling of Parzival's story is meant to draw them back to eternity and remind them that when we humble ourselves and choose to serve those we love despite our failures, shame, or guilt, it brings healing to our family and to creation itself in a way nothing else can. This reveals holiness, otherness, so that everyone can see and benefit from its potency and power. It's not some abstract devotional concept found in heady theological books about God and the Hebrew translation of words. This is eternity crashing into our space and marking us forever, regardless of what life brings us. When we remember, we behold, and when we behold, we become, and when we become, we belong. Look at your life, your story. All you have probably ever wanted was simply to belong, to know you have a place and a people who welcome you, despite you.

Love Is the Purpose

In the end, this is the road every man must walk. We cannot stop in the middle of our journey; we have an obligation to engage with the story we were given, for the sake of our families and for those who come after us. This is never going to be about you and what you get out of it. There is no pursuing the Grail in your strength; there is no finding who you are and healing from your broken heart in greater religious works or feats of devotion. You must face death, and you must fall in love. This is the quest, and in those humbling experiences a thousand times over you will be formed into a man who can offer love and receive love.

This isn't possible for men who have not faced death and come to the end of themselves. Only there can you find what you are looking for. Only there will you glimpse the Grail and find God in any real way.

Love is the purpose, and not just a love that benefits you, but a love that destroys you and puts you back together again. It is with great love and the acceptance of death that we are able to see this journey through all the way to the end, and there is no greater love we can experience than the love of Christ in the midst of our failures.

THE WORK

What does it look like for you to rest? Enjoying a true Sabbath once each week? Taking a few weeks of vacation with your family? Practicing some of the meditation skills we reviewed earlier in this book? Ask yourself how you rest and recharge and schedule time to truly rest and reflect on the life God has entrusted to you. Remember that you are on a journey. This is just the end of a book, but your life, your spouse, your children are all waiting for you to become the man you were meant to become. So slow down this week, show yourself kindness, and remember Sabbath. This is all you need right now.

Sabbath is the greatest work you can do when you find yourself in the throes of a long journey. Sabbath is more than a day off; it is agreement that God has it all under control. The fullness of your journey was set by Him and for Him so in Sabbath, we recognize His authority and put our trust in Him. Sabbath is a form of worship that has been long neglected in most men in the name of efficiency, telling the world they "are so busy" and have "so much to do" but neglecting rest and the work of the soul that can only come when we let God be God and we embrace the finite nature of our experience here. Take a deep breath; don't try to accomplish in twenty hours or twenty days what should take twenty years. You are doing great; the journey ahead as you continue to walk these paths toward biblical masculinity will come with much beauty and much brokenness, but you are not alone.

Appendix I

The "I Am" List

I am given better than I deserve because of God's love for me.	Psalm 103:10–12
I am redeemed from the hand of the adversary.	Psalm 107:2
I am carried through by God Himself.	Isaiah 46:4
My sinful nature has been healed in Jesus.	Isaiah 53:5
I am the salt of the earth.	Matthew 5:13
I am the light of the world.	Matthew 5:14
I am commissioned to make disciples, and Christ is with me always.	Matthew 28:19–20
I am a child of God.	John 1:12; Romans 8:16–17; 1 John 3:1–2
I have eternal life.	John 3:16
I have been given peace.	John 14:27
I am part of the True Vine.	John 15:1–5
I am clean.	John 15:3
I am Jesus' friend.	John 15:15
I am chosen and appointed by Jesus to bear fruit.	John 15:16
I have been given glory; I am one with Jesus.	John 17:22
I am justified.	Romans 5:1
I died with Christ and died to the power of sin's rule over my life.	Romans 6:1–6

I am a slave of righteousness.	Romans 6:18
I am set free from sin and enslaved by God.	Romans 6:22
I am free from condemnation.	Romans 8:1
I am led by the Spirit of God.	Romans 8:14
I am a son of God.	Romans 8:14–15; Galatians 3:26; 4:6
I am an heir of God and a coheir with Christ.	Romans 8:17
I am more than a conqueror through Christ, who loves me.	Romans 8:37
I am being transformed by the renewing of my mind.	Romans 12:2
I am sanctified and called to holiness.	1 Corinthians 1:2
I am a saint.	1 Corinthians 1:2; Ephesians 1:1; Philippians 1:1; Colossians 1:2
I have been given grace.	1 Corinthians 1:4
I have been placed into Christ by God's doing.	1 Corinthians 1:30
I have received the Spirit of God into my life, that I might know the things given to me by God.	1 Corinthians 2:12
I have been given the mind of Christ.	1 Corinthians 2:16
I am a temple, a dwelling place of God. His Spirit and His Life dwell in me.	1 Corinthians 3:16; 6:19
I am united to the Lord, and I am one in spirit with Him.	1 Corinthians 6:17
I am not my own; I have been bought with a price, and I belong to God.	1 Corinthians 6:19–20; 7:23
I am called by God.	1 Corinthians 7:17
I am a member of Christ's Body.	1 Corinthians 12:27; Ephesians 5:30
I am victorious.	1 Corinthians 15:57
I have been established, anointed, and sealed by God in Christ, and have been given the Holy Spirit as a pledge guaranteeing my inheritance to come.	2 Corinthians 1:21–22; Ephesians 1:13–14
I am led by God in triumphal procession.	2 Corinthians 2:14

I am a fragrance of Christ to God among those who are being saved and among those who are perishing.	2 Corinthians 2:15
I am being changed into the likeness of Jesus.	2 Corinthians 3:18
I am living by faith and not by sight	2 Corinthians 5:7
I no longer live for myself, but for the One who died and rose again on my behalf.	2 Corinthians 5:14–15
I am a new creature.	2 Corinthians 5:17
I am reconciled to God, and I am a minister of reconciliation.	2 Corinthians 5:18–19
I have been made righteous.	2 Corinthians 5:21
I am well content with weaknesses . . . for when I am weak, then I am strong.	2 Corinthians 12:10
I have been crucified with Christ, and it is no longer I who live, but Christ lives in me.	Galatians 2:20
I am redeemed from the curse of the law.	Galatians 3:13
I am heir to the blessing of Abraham.	Galatians 3:14
I am a son of God through faith in Christ Jesus.	Galatians 3:26
I am Abraham's seed, and heir of the promise from God.	Galatians 3:29
I am no longer a slave, but a son, and if a son, then an heir through God.	Galatians 4:6–7
I am blessed with every spiritual blessing.	Ephesians 1:3
I was chosen before the foundation of the world, that I would be holy and blameless before God.	Ephesians 1:4
I am adopted as a son through Jesus Christ to God the Father.	Ephesians 1:5
I am forgiven.	Ephesians 1:7
I am sealed with the Holy Spirit of promise.	Ephesians 1:13
I am alive together with Christ.	Ephesians 2:5
I have been raised up with Christ, and I am seated with Him in heavenly places.	Ephesians 2:6
I am given faith. I am saved by grace, through faith.	Ephesians 2:8
I am God's workmanship, created in Christ Jesus for good works.	Ephesians 2:10

I have access in one Spirit to the Father.	Ephesians 2:18
I am a fellow citizen with the saints, and I am of God's household.	Ephesians 2:19
I have boldness and confident access to God through faith in Him.	Ephesians 3:12
I am an imitator of God, as a beloved child who walks in Jesus' love.	Ephesians 5:1–2
I am strong in the Lord and in His mighty power.	Ephesians 6:10
I am a citizen of heaven.	Philippians 3:20
I am capable. I do all things through Christ who strengthens me.	Philippians 4:13
I have been rescued from the domain of darkness and transferred to the Kingdom of God's beloved Son.	Colossians 1:13
I am redeemed.	Colossians 1:14
I am blameless and free from accusation.	Colossians 1:22
Christ Himself is in me.	Colossians 1:27
I am firmly rooted in Jesus, and I am being built up in Him.	Colossians 2:7
I have been made complete in Jesus.	Colossians 2:10
I have been spiritually circumcised; my old unregenerate nature has been removed.	Colossians 2:11
I have been buried, raised, and made alive in Jesus.	Colossians 2:12–13
I died with Christ and have been raised up with Christ. My life is now hidden with Christ in God. Christ is now my life.	Colossians 3:1–4
I am chosen of God, holy and dearly loved.	Colossians 3:12
I am a son of light and not of darkness.	1 Thessalonians 5:5
I have been given a spirit of power, love, and self-discipline.	2 Timothy 1:7
I have been saved and set apart, according to God's doing.	2 Timothy 1:9; Titus 3:5
Because I am sanctified and I am one with the Sanctifier, He is not ashamed to call me brother.	Hebrews 2:11
I am a holy partaker of a heavenly calling.	Hebrews 3:1

I have the right to come boldly before the throne of God to find mercy and grace in time of need.	Hebrews 4:16
I have been born again.	1 Peter 1:23
I am a living stone, being built up as a spiritual house to be a holy priesthood, to offer up spiritual sacrifices acceptable to God through Jesus Christ.	1 Peter 2:5
I am a member of a chosen race, a royal priesthood, a holy nation, a people for God's own possession.	1 Peter 2:9
I am an alien and stranger in this world.	1 Peter 2:11
I am healed by Christ's wounds.	1 Peter 2:24
I am an enemy of the devil.	1 Peter 5:8
I am a partaker of God's divine nature, having been given His exceedingly great and precious promises.	2 Peter 1:4
I am forgiven on account of Jesus' name.	1 John 2:12
I am anointed by God.	1 John 2:27
I am loved by God.	1 John 4:10
I am an heir of eternal life.	1 John 5:11
I have life.	1 John 5:12
I am born of God; the evil one (the devil) cannot touch me.	1 John 5:18
I have been ransomed by Christ's blood for God.	Revelation 5:9
I am an overcomer by the blood of the Lamb and the word of my testimony.	Revelation 12:11

Appendix II

The Genogram

The illustration included here is what a basic genogram looks like. Each genogram will be unique to the individual and gives you a visual representation of your family history, including major events, health, faith, and relational dynamics. Follow these steps to draw your own genogram:

Step 1: Draw all the people in your family line just two generations back, from you to your grandparents, on both sides if you are married. Give yourself plenty of space to write details and draw around them (using a standard 8.5 x 11 piece of paper might be best). If there are divorces and step-parents, include all of them on the image, using squares for men and circles for women. Then inside those shapes, include the family members' age if they are alive, and an X if they have passed away. Once you have finished that, follow the remaining instructions for steps 2, 3, and 4.

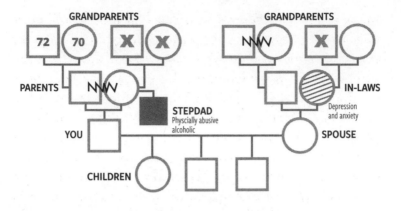

Step 2: Focus on relational connections. I want you to draw a zigzag line wherever there was divorce or adultery. In the space around that shape, write which it was.

Step 3: Focus on abuse (physical, emotional, verbal), plus addiction (drugs, sex, alcohol). I want you to fill in any shapes that represent for you the individuals with those experiences. In the space around each shape, write what it was.

Step 4: Focus on health challenges, both physical (cancer, chronic pain, disease, deformities) and mental (depression, suicide, anxiety, eating disorders, bipolar disorder, mental disabilities). I want you to draw lines through the shapes that represent those individuals in your family who have struggled with these physical and mental health challenges. In the space around each shape, write specifically what those challenges were.

You are now looking at a very basic image of what your family has experienced. This is what you were handed as a child and what you brought into your marriage, if you are married.

Many genogram resources would also include several more things, which I encourage you to continue to research. But for now, I just want you to grab your journal and write down any patterns you noticed within the image of your genogram as you are stumbling forward in immaturity. Are there cycles you can see in your family line that you are currently dealing with? Write down anything of interest that you can explore further at another time. Include what emotions each layer of the image brings you. Do you have any emotional or physical reaction when looking at specific individuals in your family line, or in your spouse's line? Take the time to explore your feelings and reactions, and see what arises. Make sure to write all of it in your journal.

Appendix III

The Story Map

Grab a piece of paper and four colored markers or colored pencils, whatever you can find. Then get alone with your thoughts, because this story map will take some effort. Draw lines on your paper like the ones in the illustration that follows. The vertical line with the numbers on the left side represents the effect of your experiences, 0 to +10 being positive, and 0 to -10 being negative. This is all subjective based on your experience; you're not comparing it to someone else's experience. The horizontal line through the center represents your life in chronological order, the left being your childhood, following to the right up to today. Our goal is to focus on the "formative years" of your life between the ages of 4 and 18. There are many things that could have happened after the age of 18, but you will find that most root systems for those experiences are found within the most formative years of your life, the years under 18. Once you have drawn out the lines, follow the directions below.

The image at the end of this exercise gives you a rough idea of what your story map will look like as you develop it. As you fill

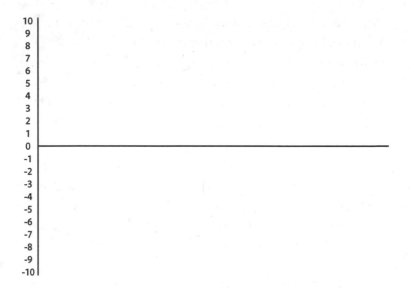

in your map, we're going to focus on four key areas of your life experience and see where there are patterns and where there are points for further exploration. Your goal is not to be thorough, so much as to be curious. Don't get caught up too much in the emotion at this point; simply mark each memory and write a small note about what happened and your age at the time.

The four key areas we will divide our exploration into are *family of origin*, *faith*, *relationships* (both friends and romantic), and *sexuality*. Each area gets a specific color and a new line as we map our experiences. Begin with your family of origin. From your earliest memories, begin to place markers with a circle, your age, and a small note simply for reference later.

Then do the same with a new color for faith experiences, marking where you first met God, where in your life you've seen Him work, where you were amazed by His love or provision, where you felt His presence.

Now, with another color mark significant experiences with friends and romantic relationships outside your family of origin.

Who were the significant peers and young loves in your life? What marking moments taught you about life and love through those whom you spent time with? What did you learn through these experiences about your position in the world and about how to engage with dating and love?

Finally, in one last color mark significant moments in discovering and experiencing your sexuality. When did you first realize your desire for sex and mutual attraction? Did you have someone to talk to? Did you find your sexuality in unhealthy ways? Were you taken advantage of? Or were you given healthy experiences and expectations?

The goal of this story map exercise, like a genogram, is exploration so you can begin to understand and gain perspective on your experiences—the positive and negative events that formed you into who you are today. Take time in your journal to explore each dot, each circle with curiosity. Give each marked moment more details, and begin to see how it makes you feel emotionally and physically.

In the context of our earlier discussions about male initiation, I want you to ask yourself the following questions about the work you just did:

1. *What did I learn to do with my pain based on these experiences?*
   Looking at this map, can you see where you learned this?

2. *What happened to the crown I was given when I was born?*
   Did you have someone to trust that you handed it to, or was it lost, stolen, or forgotten? Where in your story can you see what happened?

3. *Are there patterns in my story that I noticed by doing this work?*

What can you see, and how has it defined who you are today?

4. *What were the seasons of my greatest joy, and what were the seasons of my greatest pain?*

Can you define why, based on the map you created?

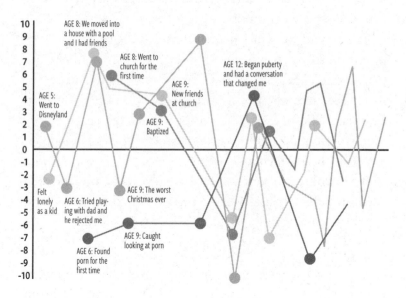

Appendix IV

Emotions and Sensations List

Peaceful

Related feeling words: Calm ▾ Caring ▾ Centered ▾ Content ▾ Encouraged ▾ Expectant ▾ Fulfilled ▾ Optimistic ▾ Patient ▾ Reflective ▾ Relaxed ▾ Serene ▾ Trusting ▾ Vulnerable ▾ Warm

Joyful

Related feeling words: Amazed ▾ Awed ▾ Blissful ▾ Delighted ▾ Eager ▾ Ecstatic ▾ Enchanted ▾ Energized ▾ Engaged ▾ Enthusiastic ▾ Excited ▾ Free ▾ Happy ▾ Inspired ▾ Invigorated ▾ Lively ▾ Passionate ▾ Playful ▾ Radiant ▾ Refreshed ▾ Rejuvenated ▾ Renewed ▾ Satisfied ▾ Thrilled ▾ Vibrant

Angry

Related feeling words: Aggravated ▾ Agitated ▾ Annoyed ▾ Bitter ▾ Contemptuous ▾ Cynical ▾ Disdainful ▾ Disgruntled ▾ Disturbed ▾ Edgy ▾ Exasperated ▾ Frustrated ▾ Furious ▾ Grouchy ▾ Hostile ▾ Impatient ▾ Irate ▾ Irritated ▾ Moody ▾ Outraged ▾ Resentful ▾ Upset ▾ Vindictive

Confident

Related feeling words: Adventurous ▾ Brave ▾ Capable ▾ Courageous ▾ Daring ▾ Determined ▾ Free ▾ Grounded ▾ Powerful ▾ Proud ▾ Strong ▾ Valiant ▾ Worthy

Present

Related feeling words: Accepted ▾ Affectionate ▾ Caring ▾ Compassion ▾ Empathetic ▾ Fulfilled ▾ Loved ▾ Present ▾ Safe ▾ Seen ▾ Warm ▾ Worthy

Curious

Related feeling words: Aroused ▾ Engaged ▾ Fascinated ▾ Interested ▾ Intrigued ▾ Involved

Sad

Related feeling words: Anguished ▾ Depressed ▾ Despondent ▾ Disappointed ▾ Discouraged ▾ Forlorn ▾ Gloomy ▾ Grieved ▾ Heartbroken ▾ Hopeless ▾ Lonely ▾ Longing ▾ Melancholy ▾ Sorrowful ▾ Teary ▾ Unhappy ▾ Upset ▾ Weary ▾ Yearning

Numb

Related feeling words: Aloof ▾ Bored ▾ Confused ▾ Disconnected ▾ Distant ▾ Empty ▾ Indifferent ▾ Isolated ▾ Lethargic ▾ Listless ▾ Removed ▾ Resistant ▾ Uneasy ▾ Withdrawn

Fearful

Related feeling words: Anxious ▾ Apprehensive ▾ Frightened ▾ Hesitant ▾ Nervous ▾ Panicked ▾ Paralyzed ▾ Scared ▾ Terrified ▾ Worried

Grateful

Related feeling words: Appreciative ▾ Blessed ▾ Delighted ▾ Fortunate ▾ Graced ▾ Humbled ▾ Lucky ▾ Moved ▾ Thankful ▾ Touched

Anxious

Related feeling words: Burned-out ▾ Cranky ▾ Depleted ▾ Edgy ▾ Exhausted ▾ Frazzled ▾ Impotent ▾ Incapable ▾ Overwhelmed ▾ Rattled ▾ Rejected ▾ Resigned ▾ Restless ▾

Shaken ▾ Stressed ▾ Tense ▾ Tight ▾ Trapped ▾ Victimized ▾ Weary

Worried

Related feeling words: Apprehensive ▾ Concerned ▾ Dissatisfied ▾ Disturbed ▾ Doubtful ▾ Grouchy ▾ Hesitant ▾ Inhibited ▾ Perplexed ▾ Questioning ▾ Rejected ▾ Shocked ▾ Skeptical ▾ Suspicious ▾ Ungrounded ▾ Unsure

Shameful/Guilty

Related feeling words: Fragile ▾ Helpless ▾ Humiliated ▾ Inhibited ▾ Mortified ▾ Regretful ▾ Remorseful ▾ Self-conscious ▾ Sorry ▾ Useless ▾ Weak ▾ Worthless

Body Sensations List

Achy	Expanded	Numb	Spacey
Airy	Flowing	Painful	Spacious
Blocked	Fluid	Pounding	Sparkly
Breathless	Fluttery	Prickly	Stiff
Bruised	Frozen	Pulsing	Still
Burning	Full	Queasy	Suffocated
Buzzy	Gentle	Radiating	Sweaty
Clammy	Hard	Relaxed	Tender
Clenched	Heavy	Releasing	Tense
Cold	Hollow	Rigid	Throbbing
Constricted	Hot	Sensitive	Tight
Contained	Icy	Settled	Tingling
Contracted	Itchy	Shaky	Trembly
Dizzy	Jumpy	Shivery	Twitchy
Drained	Knotted	Slow	Vibrating
Dull	Light	Smooth	Warm
Electric	Loose	Soft	Wobbly
Empty	Nauseous	Sore	Wooden

Notes

Path 2 Stepping into a Bigger Story

1. Martin Shaw, *Courting the Wild Twin* (London: Chelsea Green Publishing UK, 2020), back cover text.

2. Rod Dreher, "Martin Shaw's Miraculous Conversion," *The American Conservative*, November 12, 2022, https://www.theamericanconservative.com/martin-shaws-miraculous-conversion/.

3. *Merriam-Webster Unabridged Dictionary Online*, s.v. "parable," accessed January 2, 2024, https://unabridged.merriam-webster.com/collegiate/parable.

4. Irvin D. Yalom, *Love's Executioner and Other Tales of Psychotherapy* (New York: Basic Books, Perseus Books Group, 2012), xxii.

Path 3 Embracing Where You Came From

1. For an incredible video about this that's worth the watch, see Big Think's "Male inequality, explained by an expert," featuring Richard Reeves, author of the book *Of Boys and Men*. You can find the video at https://www.youtube.com/watch?v=DBG1Wgg32Ok.

2. National Center for Fathering (NCF), "The Extent of Fatherlessness," accessed January 3, 2024, https://fathers.com/the-extent-of-fatherlessness/#:~:text=More%20than%2020%20million%20children,attention%20as%20a%20national%20emergency.

3. Robert Bly, *Iron John: A Book about Men*, 3rd ed. (Boston: Da Capo Press, Perseus Books Group, 2015), 59.

4. Richard Shelton, "Letter to a Dead Father," in Jim Perlman, ed., *Brother Songs: A Male Anthology of Poetry* (Duluth, Minn.: Holy Cow! Press, 1979, 1996), n.p.

5. Shelton, "Letter," n.p.

Path 4 Listening to the Call of Adventure

1. Martin Shaw, *Snowy Tower: Parzival and the Wet, Black Branch of Language* (Ashland, OR: White Cloud Press, 2014), 22.

2. Theodora Blanchfield, "What Are the Mental Health Effects of Being Adopted?" Verywell Mind, last updated December 6, 2023, https://www.very wellmind.com/what-are-the-mental-health-effects-of-being-adopted-521779 9#:~:text=Adoptees%20are%20more%20likely%20to,Depression.

3. "Between Two Worlds," Center for Action and Contemplation article adapted from Richard Rohr, *Adam's Return: The Five Promises of Male Initiation* (New York: Crossroad, 2004), 135–38, April 26, 2020, https://cac .org/daily-meditations/between-two-worlds-2020-04-26/.

Path 5 Stumbling Forward in Immaturity

1. William Stafford, *Stories That Could Be True: New and Collected Poems* (New York: Harper & Row, 1982), 4.

2. This tool finds its roots in the 1970s, with one of the founders of systemic therapy, American psychiatrist and psychotherapist Murray Bowen. His work was later built upon and formalized into the genogram by family therapists Monica McGoldrick, Randy Gerson, and Sylvia Shellenberger in 1985, with a book they published called *Genograms: Assessment and Intervention.*

Path 6 Tempering Aggression through Initiation

1. Rachel Nuwer, "When Becoming a Man Means Sticking Your Hand Into a Glove of Ants," Smithsonian Magazine, October 27, 2014, https://www .smithsonianmag.com/smart-news/brazilian-tribe-becoming-man-requires -sticking-your-hand-glove-full-angry-ants-180953156/.

2. Martin Shaw, *Snowy Tower: Parzival and the Wet, Black Branch of Language* (Ashland, OR: White Cloud Press, 2014), 228.

Path 8 Encountering Divine Femininity

1. Blue Letter Bible, s.v. "'ēzer (Strong's H5828)," accessed January 4, 2024, https://www.blueletterbible.org/lexicon/h5828/kjv/wlc/0-1/. On this website, you can find a list of all the Scriptures this word appears in, if you want to look into the meaning yourself.

2. Nicholas H. Wolfinger, "Does Sexual History Affect Marital Happiness?", Institute for Family Studies (IFS), October 22, 2018, https://ifstudies .org/blog/does-sexual-history-affect-marital-happiness.

3. Janelle Hansen and Melina Rogers, "Premarital Sex and Divorce," University of Utah, July 8, 2016, https://attheu.utah.edu/facultystaff/premarital -sex-and-divorce.

Path 9 Discovering True Strength by Embracing Failure

1. Antonio Machado, *Times Alone: Selected Poems of Antonio Machado*, trans. Robert Bly (Middletown, CT: Wesleyan University Press, 2011), 113.

2. Rumi, "The Core of Masculinity," Reddit, accessed January 4, 2024, https://www.reddit.com/r/JordanPeterson/comments/67pi7y/the_core_of _masculinity_by_rumi/?rdt=33468.

Path 10 Engaging in the Redemptive Work of Grief

1. David Whyte, "The Well of Grief," found at Best Poems Encyclopedia, https://www.best-poems.net/david-whyte/the-well-of-grief.html.
2. Whyte, "Well of Grief."
3. Lana Burgess, "Eight benefits of crying: Why it's good to shed a few tears," Medical News Today, last updated July 13, 2023, https://www.medical newstoday.com/articles/319631.
4. Richard Rohr, OFM, *From Wild Man to Wise Man: Reflections on Male Spirituality* (Cincinnati, OH: Franciscan Media, 1990, 1996, 2005), Kindle edition, chapter 13.
5. American Foundation for Suicide Prevention (AFSP), "Suicide Statistics," Centers for Disease Control and Prevention (CDC) Data & Statistics Fatal Injury Report for 2021, retrieved by AFSP May 19, 2023, https://afsp .org/suicide-statistics/.
6. Fiona L. Shand, Judy Proudfoot, Michael J. Player, et. al., "What might interrupt men's suicide? Results from an online survey of men," NIH: National Library of Medicine, October 15, 2015, https://www.ncbi.nlm.nih.gov /pmc/articles/PMC4611172/.

Path 11 Learning to Integrate the Shadow

1. Robert Bly, "The Long Bag We Drag Behind Us," excerpted from Bly's *A Little Book on the Human Shadow* in *The Sun* magazine's "The Dog-Eared Page" feature, August 2012, https://static1.squarespace.com/static/5785b85b 15d5dbb0fab56c26/t/60144eb382281a648bd59bb8/1611943607009/The+Long +Bag_Bly.pdf.
2. Keith Rose, "6 Ways That Watching Porn Affects Relationships," CovenantEyes, last updated October 27, 2023, https://www.covenanteyes.com/20 22/05/18/6-ways-that-watching-porn-affects-relationships/.
3. Mary Oliver, "The Journey," found at Oprah online, https://static.oprah .com/images/201104/omag/the-journey.pdf.

Path 12 Arriving Where You Always Belonged

1. Edwin H. Zeydel, in collaboration with Bayard Quincy Morgan, *The Parzival of Wolfram von Eschenbach: Translated into English Verse with Introduction, Notes, Connecting Summaries* (Chapel Hill, NC: University of North Carolina Press, 1951), 320.
2. For more on this ministry, visit www.ThisIsTheFight.com.

JAKE HAMILTON has been a church planter, creative entrepreneur, pastor, and worship leader whose songs have been sung and recorded around the world. He is also a dynamic preacher and communicator, speaking in schools and stadiums across the globe. He has a powerful and often disruptive approach to delivering God's Word.

Jake and his wife, Nicci, have also given themselves fully to marriages and the redeeming power of reconciled relationships. He believes that reconciliation in marriages will be the catalytic force for reformation in the Church, and it begins when a man discovers who he is. His ministry to men, called The Fight, devotes itself to helping men learn what it means to walk in biblical manhood, as modeled by Jesus Christ, and also to helping them realize they are not alone as they take responsibility for their lives, stories, and families.

As an artist, Jake pushes the limits of creativity, and as a father and husband, he is committed to his family first. But above any endorsement or accomplishment, he is a lover of Jesus Christ, with the ability to lead others into the same encounter with Christ that transformed his own life. He has always said that his goal is simple: "I want to spend my life throwing keys into prison cells."

Learn more about Jake and his ministry at www.ThisIsThe Fight.com.